Your qualification may get you through the interview door, but getting your dream job requires much more.

In this book, you will discover the three key strategies for getting hired. It will show you how to identify your strongest qualities for any job interview and additionally, will provide you with the most appropriate responses to typical job interview questions. This material comes with practice worksheets that will enable you apply the key learning of the book to position you perfectly for the next dream job.

— Harry Nnoli —

# YOU'RE HIRED

## MAKING THE BEST OF JOB INTERVIEWS

*AuthorHouse™ LLC*
*1663 Liberty Drive*
*Bloomington, IN 47403*
*www.authorhouse.com*
*Phone: 1-800-839-8640*

*© 2013 by Harry Nnoli. All rights reserved.*

*No part of this book may be reproduced, stored in a retrieval system, or transmitted by any means without the written permission of the author.*

*Published by AuthorHouse    09/16/2013*

*ISBN: 978-1-4918-0265-6 (sc)*
*ISBN: 978-1-4918-0264-9 (hc)*
*ISBN: 978-1-4918-0263-2 (e)*

*Library of Congress Control Number: 2013914309*

*Any people depicted in stock imagery provided by Thinkstock are models, and such images are being used for illustrative purposes only.*
*Certain stock imagery © Thinkstock.*

*This book is printed on acid-free paper.*

*Because of the dynamic nature of the Internet, any web addresses or links contained in this book may have changed since publication and may no longer be valid. The views expressed in this work are solely those of the author and do not necessarily reflect the views of the publisher, and the publisher hereby disclaims any responsibility for them.*

# Table of Contents

Introduction ................................................................. vii

## PART I
## THE BASICS

Chapter 1: Becoming a Person of Value ......................... 3
Chapter 2: What Employers Seek When Hiring ............. 6
Chapter 3: Preparing for the Dream Job ....................... 12

## PART II
## GETTING PREPARED: THE "3R" STRATEGY

Chapter 4: Preparing for an Interview ........................... 21
Chapter 5: Rehearse ...................................................... 35
Chapter 6: Replicate ..................................................... 46

## PART III
## THE MOMENT OF TRUTH

Chapter 7: Handling Typical Interview Questions (Best Answers) ....................... 57

## PART IV
## THE OFFER AND CHOICES

Chapter 8: After the Job Interview ................................ 81

Conclusion ................................................................... 93

Appendices (A-H)

Appendix A: SWOT Analysis .......................................................... 99
Appendix B: Your 5-Star Points Approach ................................... 100
Appendix C: Your Answers to Typical Interview Questions .......... 104
Appendix D: Types of Job Interviews ........................................... 114
Appendix E: Dress Code for Job Interviews ................................. 121
Appendix F: Important Tips for Writing
 an Interview Winning Resume .................................. 126
Appendix G: Benefits of SWOT Analysis ..................................... 136
Appendix H: A Simple Breathing Exercise to Relieve Tension ........ 138

Bibliography ................................................................................. 139
About the Author .......................................................................... 141
Audio Materials for Personal Development ................................. 143

# Introduction

As a result of the recession, many people have lost their jobs, and there are many others out there looking for jobs. In the foreseeable future, it's likely that there will be more qualified people than available job positions in many industries.

The major issue is that prospective employers are not interested in offering anyone a job, because they are not looking for job seekers, rather they are searching for problem-solvers and solution-providers.

Most of the people looking for jobs will have trouble finding jobs not because they lack the necessary skills, but primarily because they lack a proper orientation. The job seeker may just want a job, but the prospective employer wants a person of value. If you are going to be successful at job-hunting, you must show that you are the right person the prospective employer is looking for.

Understand that value is not defined by semantics but in real terms; how your input to the organization can help them grow revenues, reduce cost, enhance service to the customer, and deliver the products and services of the organization in a manner that is more convenient for the consumers to access. These are the fundamental ways corporate organizations define value; it ultimately revolves around the customer and drive for profitability.

This book has been segmented into four major parts, each with necessary ingredients you need for success at the next interview. The first part establishes the fundamentals for securing that "dream job." These include defining your value proposition, writing an interview winning resume, and harnessing the power of your imagination.

The second part of the book prepares you to take on any type of job interview, helps you assess the organization and yourself, and details three key strategies for getting hired. These are indispensable to securing your dream job, whether at officer or entry-level, middle or senior management position.

The third part of the book focuses on the best answers to typical job interview questions.

The fourth and final part of the book concentrates on making the right choice after securing the job.

The appendices (A-H) afford you the opportunity to practice specifically for the interview with the worksheets provided alongside other relevant details, which you will find very useful.

Keep this book well until you become a CEO, then you can hand it over!

# PART I
## THE BASICS

CHAPTER **1**

# Becoming a Person of Value

*If a man is called to be a street sweeper, he should sweep streets even as Michelangelo painted, or Beethoven composed music, or Shakespeare wrote poetry. He should sweep streets so well that all the hosts of heaven and earth will pause to say, "Here lived a great street sweeper who did his job well."*

Martin Luther King, Jr.

Adding value to yourself is the process of investing in yourself so you can contribute more to your environment.

Like an expensive jewel in a shop, you should be worth what someone is willing to pay for you.

Improve yourself constantly: read a new book, learn a new trade, learn a new subject, learn a new sport, and invest time in upgrading your skills and knowledge.

One of the best ways to find a job is to do an excellent job in the one you have, even if it's not the ideal job you want. Always "think fresh," and challenge yourself to come up with alternatives and options to a problem. This way you will always train yourself to be a solution-provider. Learn something new every day, and make up your mind not to give half measure on your job.

Be someone your employer knows to do more than you are paid for. Open your mind to new ideas and always be ready to challenge the status quo. Always be willing to help, and be disposed to teach others when you have knowledge, skills, and ability that others do not have. People hoard information because they think that the other person may become better than they are. Well, each time you teach another person, you also learn and become better. Those you teach will never beat you unless you stop learning.

If you are currently without a job, don't feel locked out. It's an opportunity for you to read the numerous books you bought over the past few years that you have never opened. It's an opportunity to learn something new, to try new hobbies; you may just discover a new talent that could hold the key to your financial independence. While not the focus of this book, the discovery of your talent is one of the potential benefits of unemployment.

To constantly add value to yourself these are some of the questions that you should ask:

- What books have I read recently?
- What training or seminar have I attended?
- What professional journal have I read?

- What personal development site or educational internet site have I visited recently?

As a professional, it is the value that you have acquired that enables you to give value to your employer. You can only give what you have. When you develop your talent and skills, you deserve all the recognition and reward (financial and emotional) that you get. Your ability to earn more money will depend on your ability to contribute more to a greater number of people. It doesn't necessarily come by years of experience but by years of experience doing productive things and contributing value.

*Work not to be a man of success, rather work to be a man of value.*

Albert Einstein

CHAPTER 2

# What Employers Seek When Hiring

*Big jobs usually go to the men
who prove their ability to outgrow small ones.*

Ralph Waldo Emerson

Every employer desires to build a winning team, and to build a winning team you need good people. Hiring good people is hard and to hire great people is obviously brutally harder! So what do prospective employers look out for in the potential employees?

There are many traits looked out for by prospective employers, but here are seven that apply to any hiring decision irrespective of level or organization involved.

**1. Integrity**

People with integrity tell the truth, and keep their words. They take responsibility for their actions, admit mistakes, and fix them. They play to win the right way, by the rules. They know and adhere to the letters and the spirit that govern their companies, industry and nation. They can be relied upon.

Employers test for integrity by observing you closely as they interact with you from when you stepped into the company for the interview, how you answer the interview questions till when you leave the premises. They also test for this from outside by reputation and reference checks. The prospective employer checks to know if the candidate is honest, openly admits mistakes, talks about his life with equal measures of candor and prudence.

Some of the words synonymous with integrity include candor, honesty, forthrightness, principle and sincerity. Therefore, display these not just for the interview but also in all aspects of life.

**2. Intelligence**

This doesn't mean the person must be a rocket scientist or a heart surgeon. This means strong dose of intellectual curiosity; the desire and inspiration to learn and the breadth of knowledge to lead others. This could be refined and enhanced through education but note that education is not same as schooling. Many go to school but are not really educated, instead they get fixated on specific pattern of thoughts with little application. Think broadly, challenge the status quo and be disposed to new information.

Some of the words synonymous with intelligence are aptitude, alertness, agility, capacity, discernment and sagacity. All these will enhance your ability to win.

## 3. Maturity

This is not the same as chronological advancement in age. An individual is mature when he has developed the ability to withstand the heat, handle stress and setbacks, and also knows how to celebrate success when it comes with equal parts of joy and humility. Mature people respect the emotions and time of others. They are confident but not arrogant.

To test for this the prospective employer relies on reference checks, reputation and intuition.

Some of the words synonymous with maturity are wisdom, mellowness, fullness, advancement, and development. These virtues must flow from you.

## 4. Enthusiasm

This has to do with the candidate's lively interest in the job, any activity or life itself. This is what John Francis "Jack" Welch, former CEO/chairman of GE and bestselling author, referred to in his book, *Winning,* as positive energy and the ability to energize others. Those with this attribute thrive on action and relish change because they have the ability to go on and on. They make conversation easy, they are full of energy at the start of day, and they end it that way. They love life, never complain about working hard, because they love it anyway as much as they love to play.

Beyond being full of energy themselves they have the innate ability to get others revved up. This is the effect of positive energy. People who energize can inspire the team to take on the impossible and enjoy doing it. For this to happen, you must be an expert in your field with a great persuasive skill, which is nothing more than understanding the benefit of the task at hand to the one you want to energize, and communicating it so clearly that the person sees the benefit.

Some of the words synonymous with enthusiasm are energy, conviction, emotion, zest and passion among others. If you want to win, be full of enthusiasm; it has a way of affecting others.

**5. Intuition or The Edge**

This is the courage to make the tough yes-or-no decision. Anyone can look at an issue from different angles and some can analyze these angles endlessly. Always remember that effective people know when to stop assessing and intuitively make a tough call, even without the full information. Especially when interviewing for a manager position, prospective employers look out for this quality, not the manager that says, "Bring it back next week, we would take a second look at the figures."

The "next week" for such managers never seems to come as they habitually postpone indefinitely, and such people are so easily swayed by different shades of opinion. Indecision can stifle an organization and no employer wants such a person in his or her organization.

**6. Execute**

This is the ability to get the job done. You are enthusiastic and have made the tough call, now this quality helps you bring that call to life. I have interviewed several candidates that seemed to have everything in its proper place but it turned out when they where hired that nothing ever got done to completion. They spoke the right words, sounded convincing and enthusiastic, but each time fell shot in terms of results. The ability to execute was lacking.

From experience and by intuition an interviewer can discern people lacking in this all-important quality. They can see through the smooth and tough talking performances during the interview by drilling into the details of the candidate's previous achievements.

Those that *execute* are the people who know how to put decision into action and push them forward to completion, through persistence that overruns resistance, chaos and obstacles.

People who can execute know that winning is all about results. To execute is synonymous with eliminate, do, finish, liquidate, and carry out with respect to a task or assignment.

7. **Passion**

By passion I mean that desire, deep hunger, heartfelt excitement about work. Passionate people care about friends, colleagues and other employees winning. They are eager to learn and grow, and love it when those around them do the same and win.

Prospective employers know that a man of passion and conviction is unstoppable no matter the task. While I can send a staff on training to gain functional knowledge in any discipline in the organization, I have found from experience that it is practically near impossible to train a staff lacking in passion to become passionate. When staff are passionate, organizations can literally move mountains, and employers know this, and look out for it when they interview job candidates.

Some of the words synonymous with passion are affection, dedication, eagerness, intensity and excitement. Let these be part of your traits because the interviewer and other circumstances of life will demand for them.

With these seven attributes—integrity, intelligence, maturity, enthusiasm, intuition, execute and passion—you are armed with the knowledge that should serve as a guide when you prepare for an interview.

# CHAPTER 3

# Preparing for the Dream Job

*Never tell me the sky's the limit
when there are footprints on the moon.*

Author Unknown

## Before the Job Interview

A job interview is your chance to show a prospective employer what kind of employee he or she will get if you are hired. This is why it is essential to be well prepared for the job interview.

Preparing means being current with the industry in which you are seeking employment, so that you're familiar with the employer and aware of what he is likely to require; it means that you are well prepared to meet those needs. This will also include paying attention to details like personal appearance, mannerisms, punctuality, comportment, and demeanor.

Knowledge, especially when applied is power, and it is always your best weapon. Arm yourself with it.

A good place to start is to have a resume that commands the attention of the prospective employer, and an understanding of the basics of job interviews.

To be invited for a job interview in the first place, you typically would have made an earlier contact by applying for the job and/or by sending your resume or curriculum vitae (CV) to the prospective employer. Even when hiring managers "poach" a potential employee, they would have first received the candidate's resume or CV.

For clarity, the essential difference between a resume and a CV are the length, what is included and what each is used for. A resume, which is more popularly used, is a one or two page summary of your skills, experience and education. The CV on the other hand, is longer with more detailed synopsis. It includes a summary of your education and academic backgrounds as well as teaching, training, research, publications, awards, projects, honors, hobbies, affiliations, and other details.

In Europe, the Middle East, Africa, or Asia, employers may expect to receive a CV. In the United States, a CV is used primarily when applying for research, scientific, academic or education positions. It is also applicable when applying for fellowships or grants.

**Writing an Interview Winning Resume**
Your resume needs to be professional and polished, because if you don't have a professional resume, your application probably won't be considered by a hiring manager.

Part of writing a professional resume includes paying attention to vital details such as the use of basic fonts, indicating all relevant contact information, and incorporating keywords used in the job description for the position applied to. Other details include, choosing the appropriate formats—a lot of templates and formats are readily available online and are free—as well as prioritizing your content to match the job requirements and leveraging on technology.

If your resume requires enhancement or if you don't have any at all, then you would need to turn to appendix F page 126 right away for the tips on writing an interview winning resume.

Today's harsh economic realities have forced many longtime employees into the job market again, dusting off resumes for the first time in years. As thousands of these new candidates vie for a dwindling number of positions, recruiters are increasingly turning to talent management technology to help narrow the pool of applicants and find the best candidates for open positions. Therefore, in writing a resume you should be mindful that your resume might be reviewed by software as well as by hiring managers.

In the appendix you will find the essential elements you need to consider when writing your resume so that it puts you in a good position for the interview.

## Types of Job Interviews

A good resume puts you in a place of opportunity to be identified, and shortlisted for an interview. However, it's important that you have some general knowledge about the different types of job interviews.

There are several types of interviews you might face, but the key types are the Screening Interview, the Phone Interview, the Selection Interview, the Group Interview (or Group Selection Interview), the Panel Interview, the Presentation Interview, and the Stress Interview.

The focus of this book is primarily on Panel Interviews, which constitute about 70 percent of the interviews conducted for entry-level and middle management positions. Group and Presentation Interviews are also often an integral part of the interview process. See appendix D page 114 for notes on all seven types of job interviews.

**The Group Interview**
In the Group Interview, several job candidates are questioned at the same time. The group could be given a topic to discuss or a simple project or a game to play while the interviewers watch directly or remotely. In some cases, the Group Interview precedes a Panel Interview or a Presentation Interview.

The Group Interview is an exercise the prospective employer conducts to see how well you communicate with others and solve problems. Since any group naturally stratifies into leaders and followers, the interviewer can easily determine which category each candidate belongs, whether you are a team player, and whether the personality traits you display during the group interaction fit in well with the values of the organization. If you find yourself in this scenario, you should just act naturally, as acting like a leader or a team player if you are not one may get you a job that is inappropriate for you. As a rule, employers seek team players rather than shooting stars. **Train yourself to be a team player if you want to win in the corporate environment.**

The following tips will be helpful during Group Interviews:

1. Be friendly with other members of the group.

2. Show respect for everyone's opinion, even if you don't agree with them.

3. Do not be either domineering or docile.

4. Be lively, positive, and active.

5. If none of the interviewers is present in the interview room, you can be sure they are watching from a remote location! Show the best of yourself, and do not say or do what you would not say or do if the interviewers were present.

6. If the group gets rowdy, look out for the best way to bring order to the proceedings. For example, if everyone is talking at the same time and some (as is always the case) are more vocal than others, find a way to suggest that the team appoint a timekeeper or institute a time check. Suggest that the group have "ground rules" to guide conduct, including how long each person should talk, so everyone gets an opportunity to express himself or herself. Part of your ground rules may be that cell phones ringers be turned off, that no one should be hushed while speaking, and that those who want to express their views should so indicate by raising their hands. This kind of conduct, well-executed, will impress the interviewers and will position you favorably. Of course, there are other suggestions you may think of that could work in the situation.

7. Be confident and unassuming.

8. Keep your comments concise, and to the point. The "KISS" (Keep It Short and Simple) principle works well in group interviews.

**The Panel Interview**

In a Panel Interview, several people interview the candidate at once, so it can be intimidating. Remembering a few tricks can help you remain calm. Try to establish rapport with each member of the panel, and make eye contact with those on the panel, especially the person whose questions you are answering. In addition to what you will learn in subsequent chapters of this book about Panel Interviews, one of the ways to establish rapport with the panel is to find opportunities to highlight the strengths of the organization without resorting to empty flattery. One way to do this is to point out what the organization is doing better than its competitors and to mention how you can help the organization maximize this advantage.

For brief descriptions of the other types of interviews and suggestions on presentation skills, please see appendix D page 118.

# The Power of Imagination

If you are currently unemployed or if you want to secure a bigger or better job, begin to see yourself in the new job or new position.

Studies have shown that the human mind does not differentiate between vivid imagination and practical experience. This means that if you can visualize the job in your mind, you can have it! You can attract to yourself that job you desire by creating an imagery of it in your mind. In other words, if you can see it, you can have it. When you visualize yourself in a job in this manner, you will be more confident during the interview.

Have the right attitude ever before going for the interview. Dress for the new job, imagine yourself in that job, and conduct yourself accordingly. You attract to yourself that which you focus your mind on; your imaginative power is your creative ability.

# PART II
## GETTING PREPARED: THE "3R" STRATEGY

CHAPTER **4**

# Preparing for an Interview

*One important key to success is self-confidence. An important key to self-confidence is preparation.*

Arthur Ashe

The "3R" Strategy is essential in preparing for an interview. The first "R" is to *research* the company so you can engage the panel intelligently and confidently. The second "R" is to *rehearse.* Rehearse what you have researched that is relevant to the interview. At this stage you play out (act and talk) the interview, as you want it to turn out. This leads to the third "R" which is to *replicate*. Finally, you put in your best to replicate all that you have rehearsed when you eventually get on the "hot seat." In replicating or reproducing what you rehearsed, its important to remember what the prospective employer is looking for, and to acquaint yourself with the common mistakes to avoid at interviews discussed in the next chapter.

## Research

Before you go on a job interview, it's important to find out as much as you can about the company. That way you'll be prepared both to answer interview questions and to ask the interviewer questions. You will also be able to find out whether the company and its values are a good fit for you.

The interviewer expects you to know something about the company and the position for which you have applied. Such knowledge goes to demonstrate your true desire and aspiration to work with the organization.

A properly conducted research equips you with better insights about the company, enables you to assess the company using one of the tools (SWOT Analysis) we shall be discussing in this chapter and identifies the need or gap the organization has that you can meet with your skills.

The next thing to do is to identify your 5-point plan, referred to later in this chapter as your 5-Star Point Approach (5-SPA), which is a list of your key skills and accomplishments.

Make a list and be ready to describe your personal and professional strengths, your transferable skills, and your relevant accomplishments. These are described in detail in this chapter and the next. Your *research* should have identified qualities the company values so you can show that you have some or all of those qualities. Here are ways to research the company.

## Research The Company First

This is what I advice, use the internet to discover as much information as you can about the company. Here are suggestions on how to research a company.

**Visit the Company Website**
Visit the About Us section of the company's website, review the company's mission statement and history, as well as information about the company's values, management, products and services.

**Use Professional Network Websites**
Check the company's profile on professional network websites such as LinkedIn; they are a good way to find more information on a company you're interested in. You'll be able see your connections at the company, new hires, promotions, jobs posted, related companies, and company statistics. Take a look at your interviewer's profile to get insight into their job and their background.

You can also check several professional advisory sites to find out what candidates for the positions you are interviewing for were asked, and get advice on how tough the interview was. You will find *Handling Typical Interview Questions* discussed in chapter 7 a valuable aid in tackling questions you would most likely be asked.

**Use of Social Media**
It is recommended that you become a fan of the company on social media platforms like Facebook and Yookos, and follow it also on Yookos or Twitter. You'll find information especially on current events in and around the company that you may not have found otherwise.

**Search Engines**
Several Search Engines such as Google, Yahoo etc., and their news platforms have valuable information on companies— use them.

## Importance of Contacts

To gather useful information and gain insights into the company, who you know in the company really does matter. Here's how to use your contacts and connections to get an insider information so you can impress the interviewer and ace the interview.

**Your Social Network Connections**
Social networking websites for people with professional occupations provides you a viable platform to research information about the company. Online professional directories for individuals and businesses such as LinkedIn, offer useful information about individuals and companies for job seekers. The more connections you have on some of these professional websites, the better your chances of having a connection that can help with your job search.

Through such professional websites, you may come in contact with an existing employee of the company, or someone that's well connected with the company who could help your application for the job. These contacts may be able to refer you to the human resources or hiring manager or give you a recommendation that will help your application.

Companies use these network websites for recruiting, and providing company information to prospective employees by posting updates about the company and job listings. The easiest way to find the company's page is to search the network's "Companies" section by company name or keyword specified by the directory.

**Other Network Connections**
When you're applying for jobs, be sure to use the connections you have on different (social) networks such as community association, church, alumni, etc. If you're a college student or alumnus ask your Career Services or Alumni Office if they can give you a list of alumni who work at the company. Then send an email, or a message via any relevant social network, or call and ask for assistance.

## What is a SWOT Analysis and Why Use It?

SWOT analysis is an invaluable research tool available to you before the interview that would enhance your preparation.

SWOT is an assessment technique and an acronym for **S**trength, **W**eakness, **O**pportunity, and **T**hreat. It is a tool originally developed for business and industry, but equally useful for a product, place or person because of its simplicity and diverse application. It identifies the internal **s**trengths, and **w**eaknesses of an organization or individual, and maps them against the external **o**pportunities and **t**hreats in the market.

Specifically, SWOT is a straightforward model that assesses what an organization or an individual can and cannot do as well as the potential opportunities and threats.

**SWOT as Your Research Tool**
When using SWOT as an aspect of your *research* of an organization or for assessment of your personal capacity, remember to be specific by avoiding gray areas and always analyze in relation to the competition.

Keep your SWOT analysis short and simple, and avoid complexity and over-analysis since much of the information is subjective. I advice that you use it as a guide and not a prescription.

Typically, SWOT is used mostly in corporate organizations. I have discussed it here because it can help you assess your suitability for the job you are being interviewed for and you'll find it invaluable when considering your strengths in relation to the job. It would most importantly help you analyze the company more professionally and intelligently. Hiring managers are impressed to know that a candidate has spent some time studying the company with a view to proffering suggestions on how to fill any identified gaps in the business or department. Lets go over the components again:

- **S**trengths: characteristics of the business, project or individual that give it or him an advantage over others.
- **W**eaknesses: characteristics that place the business or individual at a disadvantage relative to others.
- **O**pportunities: elements in the environment that the business, project or individual could exploit to its or his advantage.
- **T**hreats: elements in the environment that could pose a problem for the business, project or individual.

What strengths do you perceive the company has which it has not leveraged to exploit the opportunities in the market or what strengths do you possess that you can use to help the company take advantage of the opportunities in the market or eliminate the threats in the market or shore up a perceived weakness?

For benefits of SWOT and when to apply it please see appendix G page 136

To illustrate SWOT analysis, please consider the sample table below:

|  | Internal | | External | |
|---|---|---|---|---|
|  | Strengths | Weaknesses | Opportunities | Threats |
| Industry (Tourism) | 1. Good Infrastructure.<br><br>2. Good cultural relationship with neighboring countries.<br><br>3. Initiatives for Green destination. | 1. Lack of accessibility and isolated.<br><br>2. Poor customer service.<br><br>3. Less variety of foods. | 1. Strengthening eco-tourism and growing market.<br><br>2. Development of new tourism and related products.<br><br>3. Branding and positioning internationally. | 1. Competition from other destinations.<br><br>2. Inconsistencies in government policies. |
| Company (Consulting) | 1. Reputation in marketplace.<br><br>2. Expertise at partner level in human resources management (HRM) consultancy. | 1. Shortage of consultants at operating level rather than partner level.<br><br>2. Unable to deal with multi-disciplinary assignments because of size and low capacity. | 1. Well established position with a well-defined market niche.<br><br>2. Identified market for consultancy in areas other than HRM. | 1. Large consultancies operating at a minor level.<br><br>2. Other small consultancies looking to invade the marketplace. |
| Company (Food & Beverages) | 1. Strong brand with good reputation in the marketplace.<br><br>2. Wide variety of products.<br><br>3. Prioritizes staff training | 1. Low staff morale as a result of internal changes.<br><br>2. Depleted sales team because of recent restructuring and poaching of staff by competition.<br><br>3. Plant capacity has fallen. | 1. Growing consumer market with a large youth segment.<br><br>2. Rising health consciousness in selecting brand of foods.<br><br>3. New retail chain stores opening up across the country. | 1. Aggressive competitive activities; high influx of foreign direct investment in the industry.<br><br>2. Unfavorable regulatory policies. |

| | | | | |
|---|---|---|---|---|
| Individual (salesman) | 1. Three year field sales experience. | 1. Poor time management. | 1. A growing number of unemployed graduates who can use products. | 1. Possible acquisition of the company by a competitor. |
| | 2. Good communication & presentation skills. | 2. Weak objection handling; a tendency to personalize customers' objections. | 2. Increase in the number of sports viewing centers where more products can be sold. | 2. Mergers and acquisition may lead to further job losses in the market. |
| | 3. Consistent target achievement with 25% year-on-year sales growth. | | 3. Increase number of prospective employers. More stable companies due to bailout program and new start up businesses. | 3. Other qualified candidates for the job. |
| | 4. Passionate in selling situations. | | | |

In using the SWOT analysis to prepare for an interview for example as in the sample above, the salesman should show that he can use his numerous strengths especially his field sales experience to enable the food and beverage company sell aggressively into the new retail chain stores across the country.

He should be able to show, based on his track record in sales that his employment by the company may well be key or a step in the right direction to increasing plant capacity. The possibilities you can think of in the above sample are all there to be explored and these underline the value of SWOT analysis.

## Research Yourself

After carrying out an in-depth research on the company, it is also essential to carry out a comprehensive research on yourself, and this brings us to the 5-Star Points Approach.

## Your 5-Star Points Approach

The 5 Star Points Approach (5-SPA) is a list of the five best reasons that a particular employer should engage you. Your 5-SPA may differ from company to company, depending on what you are being interviewed for, although it could be the same in some instances.

The 5-SPA applies to entry-level jobs as well as top management positions; the principles are the same.

The following will help in developing your 5-SPA, also refer to the notes on SWOT analysis:

**Your Achievements**
Be clear on what you have accomplished, both academically and professionally, and present them in the best way possible to show you are the person for the job. Typically, the more senior the position you are being interviewed for the greater the emphases placed on your professional accomplishments.

1. Background: If you are a new graduate, you may not have experience to refer to, but if you attended a good school and made good grades, then celebrate that in your Star Points. If you have been around for some time, your years of experience in your profession should be one of your 5-Star Points.

2. Awards: The awards you have won while on the job, or if you are fresh from school, departmental awards or an outstanding project you executed during your internship or a national service program could be one of your points.

Remember, you must sing your own praises without bragging; no one else will do it for you and the panel may get the impression that you never did anything. This is why you must seek to add value in everything you do today; it will count for you tomorrow.

You position yourself to win awards in anything you do by distinguishing yourself in any assignment that you are given, rather than wasting time. Excellence in any project may be what delivers your dream job. For example, if you are a manager, do something you can be proud to tell a prospective employer about in the way of a verifiable achievement. *Don't be content with collecting a salary at the end of the month; do more than you are paid for.*

3. Projects Executed: All successful assignments and tasks you have undertaken with your specific roles and accomplishments should be part of your 5-SPA. Also, mention the ones you may not have considered successful and the important lessons you learnt for future projects especially in relation to the job you're applying for.

**Your Experience**
Diverse industry experience is especially important for those who have been employed for some time.

If you have worked in several companies or industries, share one or two landmark experiences that are relevant to the position for which you are being interviewed. However, a high rate of job change could be an indication of instability and may jeopardize your chances of getting the job. Every employer wants to employ someone who will stick with a job for a reasonable period of time.

## Language Spoken

If you are multilingual, make it one of your points, especially if the job you are applying for entails traveling or mingling with people from different cultures. Your ability to speak a second or third language is a major barrier breaker (in the marketplace) and gives you an edge during the interview. This may give you an invaluable insight into the mentality of the people you are dealing with. Emphasize it if you have it!

Don't be quiet about your abilities, but celebrate them without appearing immodest before the panel. Be frank, reassuring, and unassuming.

## Your Knowledge of the Terrain and Market

This knowledge is usually borne out of experience. It is important that you separate your general industry/on-the-job experience from your specialized knowledge of the terrain, whether geographical, political, economic or social. For example, a salesman who has sold products over a geographical area with its peculiarities can highlight his specific knowledge of the geographical terrain, which he may not have gained simply by being in the industry for some time.

A banker who has dealt with big corporate accounts while working in the corporate banking department of his organization has an edge over another banker who spent all his time servicing retail customers, if they were both being interviewed for a corporate or investment banking position, though they may have same years of industry experience.

This attribute gives you an advantage during the interview and is applicable to any field or discipline.

## Your Disposition

Every business organization needs people in order to achieve its objectives, and business goals are best achieved when people work as a team. While individual skills and talents are important, the most essential ingredients to success in business are team play and a positive, winning attitude by members of the team. Consequently, you stand a good chance of being hired if you are able to demonstrate that you are a team player, a professional with a winning attitude, and someone with a positive "mind-sight" (your interpretation of what you see and experience).

*Your Mind-Sight*

Let me explain mind-sight with this story: two professionals were laid off from their jobs as a result of the global economic recession. The first professional became negative; started drinking, making trouble with his wife, hanging out with the wrong crowd, and eventually became depressed because in his words, "No company wants my services. I have made several attempts to find another job but no one wants to help me."

The other fellow held on to his goal of finding a better job than the one that he had lost. He had more rejections from prospective employers than the first, but he never gave up, repeating to himself, "I will be successful at the next attempt." It didn't matter what they said to him; he held on to a positive outlook, the vision of the better job he knew he could find. That was his mindset.

After months of trying, he was interviewed by a company that declined to hire him, but he said to them, "Keep your pay, but give me a space here to do something worthwhile. If you like what I do and want to keep me, great. If you don't, it's still fine, and I will move on as soon as you want me out." Reluctantly, the company agreed and the CEO warned him never to bring up any discussion about salary!

He was always the first to come to work and the last to leave, and he did whatever was asked of him to the best of his ability. Soon enough, one of the managers resigned, and the company was in dire need of a replacement. After searching high and low, they found none more suitable than this fellow who was working for no pay. He is now gainfully employed as a manager with better pay, better conditions, and a better position. This is the tale of two job seekers with different mind-sights!

It is always your mind-sight that determines how far you can go and whether your goals are possible.

In summary, anything that works for you in your quest to show that you are a man or woman of value and have something to offer should form part of your 5-SPA. We have highlighted your professional and academic achievements, your experiences relevant to position applied for, the different languages you speak, your knowledge of the market terrain and your disposition.

You could have only three key points or as many as ten, but what is important is that you are clear about what you are offering; that you *rehearse* them with a friend, a colleague, or a family member before the interview date, and be conversant with them.

The key to interview success is finding a way to bring in your 5-SPA in answering the questions you're asked.

One of the most common questions asked by human resources (HR) experts at interviews is, "Tell us about yourself."

This question is your opportunity to showcase all your 5-SPA—or at least some of them.

In 60 percent of the interviews I have conducted, I got to know which were the most suitable candidates within the first three minutes of the interview; most HR experts will tell you same. Therefore, make the most of your introduction by putting forward your strong points at the beginning of the interview.

If you haven't yet developed a 5-SPA, start by writing it out now; you will be amazed at what you will come up with. There is more in you than you may think. Go ahead and bring it out!

Please see appendix B page 100 for your 5-SPA exercise.

CHAPTER 5

# Rehearse

*Speak clearly, if you speak at all; carve every word before you let it fall.*

Oliver Wendell Holmes

The second "R" is to *rehearse* or *revise* the interview. Practice makes for continuous improvement (not necessarily perfection), and it will give you confidence and a sense of ease when you're "in the hot seat" at an interview.

## Getting Ready for Your Interview

Practice with a friend, a family member, or a career counselor, on how to confidently respond to typical interview questions (discussed in detail in chapter 7) and have a few questions ready to ask the interviewer.

This is a very important stage in your preparation for a successful interview. Carefully provide your own answers based on your research and the guide we have provided in chapter 7 on *Handling Typical Interview Questions*.

Pay attention to your dress code if the interview is in-person. If your interview would be conducted over the phone, rehearse this also and take note of the essential elements when interviewing over the phone.

When rehearsing bear in mind that the interview can take any form based on the different types of interviews discussed earlier, and contained in appendix D page 114. Irrespective of whether the interview is in-person or over the telephone, your ultimate aim is to demonstrate that you are the best candidate for the job.

**Dress Code for In-Person Job Interviews**
As part of your preparation, you need to be clear on how to dress for the interview. The first impression you make on a potential employer is about the most important one; you never get a second opportunity to make a first impression. The first judgment an interviewer makes is based on your appearance. For this reason, it is still important to dress professionally for a job interview, regardless of the work environment.

What's the appropriate dress code for an interview? You want to create a great impression the first time you meet your prospective employer. Look professional, smart, and sharp when going for an interview. As a rule, unless the employer clearly states otherwise, you should be formally dressed for your interview, even when the company has a "dress down" culture. In general, the candidate dressed in a suit and tie is going to make a much better impression than the candidate that is casually dressed. As a rule of thumb, candidates should never go for interviews dressed in jeans and t-shirt! It's not an acceptable dress code for interviews except where specifically required or stated in your invitation letter.

Please see suggested dress etiquette for both professional and business casual types of interview in appendix E page 121.

Check your clothing. Make sure it is appropriate—clean; free of tears, lost buttons, and sagging hems; and properly ironed.

If you plan to borrow clothing from a friend or to buy a new pair of shoes, do it ahead of time so you can be sure everything fits well and is clean and in good repair. Select comfortable clothes that are appropriate for the industry and the company. With comfortable clothes, you'll feel more relaxed and less worried about whether your clothing is pulling, bunching, or riding up so you can focus on your interviewers.

Regardless of whether you are dressing for a job interview or to go to work, remember that appearance and the first impression matter. Prospective employers often times have so many applicants they are considering, so they look quickly for reasons to cross you off the list. Don't give them one. Dress appropriately and make your best impression.

**Interview Accessories**
When wearing accessories to an interview, less is more. It's important not to over use the accessories and also important to choose accessories that will enhance your interview attire—not overwhelm it.

Remember this, when dressing for an interview, the quality of what you wear is more important than the quantity. One classic bracelet or ring, for example, will impress your interviewer or employer more than an armful of bangles or rings on every finger. In the same vein, a good quality leather folder will impress more than a loud, colorful bag and traditional flat shoes for ladies will impress more than a four-inch heel. Men should wear little or no jewelry other than a watch and/or wedding band. For details on interview accessories and how best to use them please see appendix E page 123.

**Rehearsing Phone Interview**
Talking on the phone is not as easy as it seems. I have always found it's helpful to rehearse by conducting a mock interview with someone familiar to you. If you can, record it so you can hear how you sound over the phone. You can use your mobile device to record the session. You will be amazed at the number of times you say "ums" and "ems" and "you knows" and "rights?" You can practice reducing them from your conversational speech.

For Phone Interviews, it is advisable you speak slowly, clearly and articulately. It is good practice to smile into the phone when you speak. Surprisingly, the warmth of a smile can be "perceived" by the interviewer. To enhance the quality of your telephone conversation it would be helpful to stand up while talking. When you stand up you align all the energy centers of your body. The tone of your voice will sound stronger and more confident. You will sound more believable and authoritative. This is not mandatory as some phone interviews may last for a long time. It is important that you are relaxed and at the same time energetic.

For details on what to do during the phone interviews and the seven key points to note please see appendix D page 114.

## The Ten Interview Mistakes to Avoid

While you rehearse, be mindful of the mistakes to avoid when being interviewed. If you would take time to prepare ahead of your interview, you wont have to worry about blunders after it.

What you say or don't say may be counted against you as you will find in the list below. So be prepared to avoid all negatives during the interview. For example, If you come to an interview chewing gum or drinking coffee, you will already have one strike against you. Too much perfume or not enough deodorant won't help either. Not being dressed appropriately will give you a second strike. Talking or texting on your cell phone or listening to an iPod while waiting to be called for the interview may be your final strike and you could be done with your candidacy before you even say a word. Worst still if you go on as a "talking box," using slangs and jargons.

There are many mistakes associated with interviews, and here are the ten most common job interview mistakes and errors a candidate can make.

**1. Inappropriate Dressing**

When being interviewed for a job, it's imperative to look professional and polished. Although your attire may vary based on the position you're applying for; for example, you should wear business casual clothing to an interview for a non-professional job. It's important to look well dressed, no matter what the company stipulates.

## 2. Lateness

Next on the list, is something you think would be obvious—being on time for your interview. Yet some candidates turn up for interviews later than the appointed time with all manner of excuses. To become successful in any endeavor, you must learn to eliminate your excuses and avoid excuses.

As a rule, check your interview location. Consider driving to the place where the interview will take place ahead of time, especially if it is not in a familiar location, so you can be sure of the building and note any parking requirements/restrictions.

Everyone knows that first impression is very important in getting a job, but you can make a bad first impression before you even arrive at your interview. When you arrive late, there is a tendency to become very anxious as a result of the increased flow of adrenaline in your system. This could make you sweaty, uncoordinated and disorganized. You definitely don't want this.

Running late not only suggests poor time management skills, but also shows a lack of respect for the company, the position, and even your interviewer.

Go the extra length to make sure that you arrive early. Planning to arrive much earlier provides you some cushion time in the event that something unforeseen comes up on your way to the interview.

## 3. Things You Don't Take to the Interview

Ditch the coffee, soft drink or soda before you enter your interview. If you need to eat something, do it before you get to the interview.

Not only is it unprofessional to enter with a drink in hand, but also during your interview, you should be focused on the task at hand: making a good impression and paying attention throughout the entire interviewing process.

Having a drink in front of you creates the opportunity for distraction—fiddling with the cup, or missing a question while taking a sip, for example. Although it may be a relatively rare possibility, bringing a drink into your interview also gives way to other unsightly accidents—like trembling hands spilling the drink on the desk, on you, or even your interviewer!

**4. Ringing Phones at the interview.**

Before you get to your interview, put your phone on silent mode. Texting during your interview is not only rude and disruptive, but it's a pretty clear message to your potential employer that getting the job is not your top priority.

For the same reasons, don't answer calls, and certainly don't make calls during the interview. To resist the temptation to check your phone, stow your phone in your bag before the interview.

**5. Not knowing anything about the company**

Have you taken the time to research the company, which could be your next employer? Not doing so is a big mistake.

Don't let your potential employer stun you with the question, "What do you know about this company?"

It's one of the easiest questions to ace, if only you do some research before your interview. I have once interviewed a candidate for a position of product manager who didn't know some of our obvious products; it was no need asking him about a new product we had recently launched. He was clueless!

Background information including company history, locations, divisions, and a mission statement are available in the "About Us" section on website of most companies. Research and note this ahead of time—it should form an integral part of your *rehearsals*, then print it out and read it over just before your interview to refresh your memory. Also check the company's page on different social media platforms especially those mentioned in the previous chapter, if they have one. Anyone you know who works in the company can help you with valuable insights.

**6. Vague Resume Facts**

As surprising as this may sound, many candidates are not sure of their employment facts with date; they talk as though someone else wrote the resume for them! Do you know where you worked and when? Here's how to avoid vague resume facts.

A thorough rehearsal helps you avoid this mistake. Even if you have submitted a resume when you applied for the job, you may also be asked to fill out a job application. Make sure you know the information you will need to complete an application including dates of prior employment, graduation dates, and employer contact information.

It's understandable that some of your older experiences may be hard to recall. Review the facts before your interview. It can be helpful to keep a copy of your resume for yourself to refer to during your interview, however, don't use it as a crutch.

Of course, you should never falsify any information on your resume. The more truthful you are with your resume, the better you will be able to discuss your past experiences during your interview. For details on how to write a professional interview winning resume please see appendix F page 126.

## 7. Not Paying Attention

It's very easy to get distracted during an interview, but if you do your best to listen to what the interviewer is asking, it will be easier to frame appropriate responses. Not listening or paying attention can cost you the job.

Don't let your mind zoom off during an interview. Make sure you are well rested, alert and prepared for your interview. Bring all of your attention to bear on the interview, shut everything else out of your mind as much as possible. "All is well with Junior and the dog at home." Even if all isn't well there's not much you can do at this moment, so focus!

Getting distracted and missing a question makes you look bad. However, it is in order to ask the interviewer to repeat a question for clarity.

If you feel your attention slipping away, make the effort to stay your mind on the interview and stay engaged. Maintain eye contact, lean forward slightly when talking to your interviewer, and make an active effort to listen effectively.

## 8. Talking Too Much

In stressful situations, as interviews often are, people tend to talk too much. There is nothing much worse than interviewing someone who goes on and on. The interviewer really doesn't need to know your whole life story. Keep your response concise, to-the-point and focused, and don't ramble; simply answer the question. Also avoid the use of slangs.

Don't get sidetracked and start talking about your personal life or other unrelated topics. No matter how warm, welcoming or genial your interviewer may be, an interview is a professional situation, not a personal one. Don't get too familiar either.

## 9. Not Being Prepared to Answer Questions

Your interviewer is probably going to ask you more than just the basics about where you worked. To get a feel of your aptitude for a job, your interviewer is going to take advantage of the allotted time and get everything he or she needs to know about you as an employee.

Don't let yourself be caught off guard. Prepare for your interview by reviewing the possible questions to expect, and how to answer them. Your rehearsal must focus primarily on handling typical interview questions as discussed in chapter 7 and any other possible questions relevant to that employer.

Be prepared with a list of questions to ask the employer so that you're ready when you are asked if you have questions for the interviewer. Details of type of questions to ask, and those not to ask during a job interview are discussed under *Handling Typical Interview Questions* in chapter 7.

## 10. Criticizing Past Employers

Don't make the mistake of badmouthing your boss or co-workers. It's sometimes a smaller world than you think and you don't know who your interviewer might know, including that boss who doesn't know anything. Please see my comments on this in *Handling Typical Interview Questions*.

When interviewing for a job, you want your employer to know that you can work well with other people and handle conflicts in a mature and effective way, rather than badmouthing your co-workers or talking about other people's incompetence.

The more you rehearse ahead of your interview using our worksheet in appendix B, the greater your confidence and likelihood to secure the job. In summary, remember to always pay close attention to your dressing, ensuring the moderate use of accessories. As part of your preparation for the interview, you must avoid interview mistakes especially the ten earlier listed in this chapter. These are, inappropriate dressing, lateness to the interview, taking unnecessary items to the interview, the nuisance of a ringing phone, not researching the company properly, and not being conversant with details of your resume. Other mistakes mentioned, which you must avoid include not paying attention to questions being asked during the interview, talking too much, not being prepared to answer and ask questions, and criticizing your current or previous employer.

At this point of your preparation, you are ready to face the interview panel.

## CHAPTER 6

# Replicate

*You can have everything in life you want, if you will just help other people get what they want.*

Zig Ziglar

Finally, the third "R" is to *replicate* or *reproduce* during the interview what you have *revised* or *rehearsed*. Be careful not to sound like you're reciting memorized or crammed lines, and avoid repetitions and clichés!

Your ability to do a good job of replicating what you have rehearsed is to ensure that you research and rehearse thoroughly and leave nothing to chance. These make you more confident during the interview. Do not assume you will say it right on the hot seat when you haven't said it right on the "warm seat" provided by your friend, colleague, family member or a career counselor.

The secret to replicating what you have rehearsed is in the repetitive practice until you work yourself into the mood of the interview situation. Rehearsing the typical interview questions in the later part of this book helps your confidence and composure.

In replicating, take care to observe to do the details contained in the next topic, *The Interview*, and avoid any of the common mistakes listed previously.

## The Interview

This is your moment of truth and your opportunity to shine. Stay focused and don't let anything distract you from your mission—to ace the interview and secure the job.

**Arrival and While You Wait**
Plan to arrive for your interview at least ten minutes before the appointed time. There are *no excuses* for being late.

Now smile and show your confidence! (You should have checked your teeth for food particles before leaving home.) Ditch the gum and turn off or silence your cell phone and other electronic gadgets in your possession.

Relax! If you're nervous, keep your palms up when you sit down to wait for the interviewer, as experts say, this lowers your blood pressure and air-dries the palms.

While waiting, look confident and busy. More than likely you'll end up in a waiting room for at least a few minutes. Write down your impressions of the company and the interview for future reference. Bring something to do and look busy, even if it's just writing notes in a notebook. No matter how tense you are, try to relax. A sample breathing exercise for relaxation is described in appendix H page 138.

When the interviewer walks in, be ready to shake hands but let the interviewer offer his or her hand first. Remember to keep purses and briefcases in your left hand so you can shake with your right hand. Your handshake should be firm—not sticky or wimpy—and avoid sweaty palms.

**What to Do in the Interview Room**
If you are called in to face a panel, be sure to knock on the door leading into the room and greet the panel in a confident and audible manner, and with a smile.

Do not sit in the chair provided unless the panel invites you to do so. If they don't, ask politely whether you may be seated.

Don't be anxious or in a hurry to do anything. If you are carrying a briefcase or a bag, place it on the floor beside the chair provided, sit down, adjust your clothing if necessary—unbutton your jacket and/or adjust your skirt over your knees—and look up at the panel with a relaxed smile in anticipation of the first question.

Establish rapport early in the interview. For example, wait for the interviewer to extend his or her hand for a handshake, but be ready to offer your hand immediately. Some experts suggest talking at the same rate and tone as the interviewer. For example, if the interviewer is speaking softly, so should you. However, it is best to be as natural as possible instead of concentrating on mirroring someone else.

## Answering Interview Questions

Be natural, let your answers flow; listen attentively to the questions asked and go straight to the point with your answers. Keep your answers concise, but elaborate where necessary.

Where appropriate during the course of the interview, acknowledge the question asked, either by a simple thank you for the question or by reinforcing the significance of the question. You can also use the questions asked to sell a strong point about you. For example:

> *"I appreciate your concern for integrity and speed on the job, especially in view of the huge sums of money paid by customers. It will interest you to know that while I was with xyz company, we had no losses in two years and were able to meet our monthly deliveries without fail."*

## Body Language

Body language says more about what you're thinking than what you say. Studies show that body language comprises 55% of the force of any response, whereas the verbal content only provides 7%, and paralanguage, or the intonation—pauses and sighs given when answering—represents 38% of the emphasis.

This means that non-verbal communication is as important, or even more important than, verbal communication. The evaluation of your non-verbal communication starts as soon as you walk into the company's lobby and continues until the interview is ended. If your non-verbal communication skills aren't up to par, it won't matter how well you answer the questions. When you prepare for the interview always remember that all details—verbal and non-verbal—are important.

*Eye Contact*
Making eye contact is very important, but make sure it comes natural. Maintain eye contact with the panel and direct your answers not only to the person who asked the question but also to all members of the panel to establish rapport and give you a confident disposition.

*Relax and Smile*
A smiling, relaxed face is very inviting. Resting your hands casually in your lap, rather than folding your arms across your chest, is also more inviting. If you normally move your hands around a lot when you speak, try to minimize this all through the interview; you don't want to look too stiff, but you don't want to look like you're a bundle of nervous energy by distracting the panel with your gesticulations.

**Say Thank You**
Be sure to thank the interviewer for the interview and acknowledge that his or her time is valuable. As a rule of thumb, always show appreciation at the end of your interview. A simple "thank you very much for the opportunity to meet with you" will work positively for you. It is appropriate to send a thank you note, text, or email. This gesture is recommended but not mandatory.

**A job interview that does not result in a job is not necessarily a failure. You can learn from the experience to improve your presentation and concentration for the next time.**

## Summary: Tips to Remember

1. Dress formally unless the prospective employer explicitly indicates otherwise. For professional positions, men should dress in suit and tie, and women in smart formal attire. For

non-professional jobs, business casual attire is acceptable. For details on appropriate dressing for interviews please see appendix E page 121.

2. Good grooming is essential. Your hair should be neat and well-styled. Your nails should be manicured and clean. Men's nails should be short, and women's nails should be a reasonable length and polished in a neutral color. Women shouldn't be heavily made up. I recommend a light use of perfume or cologne because a lot of people come with their natural body odor, which in some cases can be offensive and distracting. A light use of perfumes will improve your confidence level. Avoid heavy use of perfumes since some people find certain scents unpleasant. For details on interview accessories please see appendix E page 123.

3. If there is no usher, knock at the door before entry and shut the door quietly.

4. Walk confidently toward the interview panel and greet them audibly and with a smile.

5. Stand until invited to sit by the panel and be polite.

6. Place your briefcase beside the seat provided for you before you sit down.

7. After being seated, adjust your jacket and/or skirt, look up, and smile again!

8. Smile and nod (at appropriate times) when the interviewer is talking, but don't overdo it.

9. Answer most questions, especially the first one, with "thank you."

10. Avoid sounding desperate for the job. You must draw a line between being enthusiastic and being desperate. Show that you are passionate about the job by letting it show in your voice and eyes, but never sound desperate, and never beg for a job, no matter how difficult things may be for you at the moment. Remember your value.

11. Always maintain eye contact with the panel.

12. Be polite and keep an even tone to your speech. Don't be too loud or too quiet.

13. Listen. Pay attention, be attentive and interested.

14. Don't slouch.

15. Do relax and lean forward a little towards the interviewer so you appear interested and engaged.

16. Don't lean back. You will look too casual and relaxed.

17. Keep your feet on the floor and your back against the lower back of the chair.

18. Direct your answer not only to the person who asked the question, but also to all the members of the panel.

19. Don't interrupt.

20. Control your gesticulations when you're making a point.

21. Prepare a question to ask at the end of your interview if given an opportunity.

22. Relax! Stay calm. Keep your emotions to yourself and do not show anger or frown.

# PART III
## THE MOMENT OF TRUTH

CHAPTER 7

# Handling Typical Interview Questions (Best Answers)

*Agree to these ground rules: Be curious, conversational and real. Persuade (if you must) with constructive reasoning and don't interrupt. Listen, listen, and listen.*

Elizabeth Lesser & I

Interviews are fun yet always stressful, even for job seekers who have gone on countless interviews. The best way to reduce the stress is to be prepared. Take the time to review the standard interview questions you are most likely to be asked. We'll look at suggested answers to these typical interview questions, but the best answers reside within you and are based on your particular situation.

In order to have a successful interview, you must first do some *research* on the company so you are ready with knowledgeable answers for the interview questions that specifically relate to the company. After that, you can *rehearse* your answers to the questions I am about to share with you so you can *replicate* your answers before the interview panel.

When answering questions, speak slowly and clearly. Pause briefly before you answer a question so your answers will seem less rehearsed and you have a chance to collect your thoughts. Keep in mind that even a brief pause may seem like an eternity to you, but it's not.

1. **Tell us about yourself.**

You will encounter this opening question 99.9 percent of the time, so prepare for it. I recommend two approaches to answering this question.

- The Story Style: here you start by introducing yourself and then talk about your education, work experience (summarize these points with a view to highlighting a few of your 5-Star Points), your approach to life and work, your philosophy, etc.

  Don't bore the panel; keep your answer to no more than three minutes. If you answer this question well, the interview may as well end because most interviewers know the right candidate within the first few minutes of an interview.

- The Punch-Line Method: here you offer a razor-sharp sentence or two that set the stage for further discussions and set you apart from other candidates. This sentence (or sentences) is your unique selling proposition. A value-added statement that tells the panel who you are, your greatest strength, and the major benefit that the company will derive from this strength.

Here is an example of a typical answer:

> *"I'm a seasoned sales manager, strong in developing training programs and creative market penetration methods that have resulted in revenue growth of over 250 percent for xyz company in the past three years. In the teams I lead, every member counts."*

What a difference you've made with this statement! You have ensured that you have your interviewer's full attention. At this point, you might add:

> *"I'd like to discuss how I might be able to do something like that for you."*

The ball is now in their court, and you have begun a real discussion, as opposed to merely engaging in an interrogation process.

The key is that you must lead with your strongest benefit to the employer. Be specific, put a monetary value on your work if at all possible, and be ready with details if asked. Give an estimated value in terms of the money you've either helped to make or helped to save for your employer, irrespective of your role. Figures and numbers get people's attention!

The advantages of this approach are that you'll quickly gain their attention and interest, you'll get them to want to know more about you, you'll separate yourself from other candidates, and you'll have a better chance of being positively remembered and hired.

Please see appendix C page 104 for your relevant exercise.

## 2. Why should we employ you?

The best way to respond to this question is to give concrete examples of why your skills and accomplishments make you the best candidate for the job.

Take a few moments to compare the job description with your abilities, as well as mentioning what you have accomplished in your other positions. This is another opportunity to bring up again the qualities captured in your 5-SPA that are the most suitable for the position. You should also mention qualities the ideal person for the position you are being interviewed for should possess and show convincingly that you possess some or all of those qualities. Be positive and reiterate your interest in the company and the position.

For example, an applicant who is interviewing for a customer care position could say:

> *"I understand that the success of any business lies in providing excellent service to its customers at all times. This has been a personal passion for me, and I am personally fulfilled each time I see a satisfied customer smile or say thank you for a service rendered. I pride myself on my customer service skills and my ability to resolve what could be difficult situations. For the past two years, I have won the staff member of the year award in my department, and my center has recorded the highest level of customer retention for three years. Moreover, I am a patient person, and in customer care, it is an essential attribute especially in the business your company is in (mention the business*

*type of the prospective employer). I will be glad to contribute as a customer care executive to the growth of this company (mention the name of the company)."*

**The key is always to speak in terms of your ability, experience, and energy.**

Please see appendix C page 105 for your relevant exercise.

### 3. What work experience do you have?

If you are an entry-level candidate, note that every job you did as a student, as an intern, or during any national service program or primary assignment counts, in addition to general comments like your ability to learn quickly and accept challenges.

Typical answers that you could customize to suit your purpose include:

- *"I've had a job during every long vacation and summer since I was eighteen years old. My primary reason then for working was to have some extra spending money and reduce the financial pressure on my parents. As a result, I was able to sample different careers to see where I fit best."*

- *"As an undergraduate, I worked as an office assistant at a branch of one of the leading telecommunications companies during the long holidays. It was then that I discovered what I wanted to do in my career. It was easy and interesting to sell the company's products to walk-in customers, and I knew I would make a career in sales or marketing."*

- *"I have not had much paid work experience as a teacher, but I have devoted most of my time since leaving school to volunteer work at a public school in town (mention the school)."*

- *"I have used my time teaching children on my street during their vacation periods, no matter how short. Since I was working to complete my certification, I wanted to gain hands-on experience without worrying about finding a school that would hire me. Now that I am certified and have those volunteer hours, I feel well prepared to apply for a full-time teaching position."*

- *"My work experience has been top notch. When I completed my degree in economics, I worked as an apprentice with a very good analyst who consults for many big firms in the country. I was able to use this time to work on my MBA, which I just completed recently. Working with a good economist has made me an asset to any company that will hire me. Moreover, I am ready and quick to learn and willing to accept challenges. All of this makes me suitable to fill the role of an analyst in your organization."*

Please see appendix C page 106 for your relevant exercise.

## 4. What are your goals for the future, or where do you see yourself in the next five years?

The best way to respond to this interview question is to refer to the position and the company with which you are interviewing. Don't discuss your goals for returning to school or having a family; they are not relevant and could knock you out of contention for the job. Instead, connect your answer to the job for which you are applying.

Here is an example of a good response:

> *"My long-term goals involve growing with a well-established company like this one, where I can continue to learn, take on additional responsibilities, and contribute as much value as I can. Over the next five years I hope to have gained sufficient experience to move from a technical position to a management role."*

Then you can mention a position within the structure of the organization you aspire to have attained, no matter how ambitious. For example, if you are being interviewed for a human resources officer position, you could aspire within five years to rise to a human resources manager or even a senior manager, based on the value you expect to bring to the business. It will be safe to start answering this question with the phrase:

*"In a firm like yours I will like to . . ."*

Please see appendix C page 106 for your relevant exercise.

5. **If you were hired, what would you do differently (from what the company currently does)? In other words are there changes you would make to enhance the performance of the organization or department?**

Constructive changes make for improvement in any organizations and constantly many businesses seek individuals who will think out of the box and make a positive difference. This is what informs a question like this; it is not that the company is looking for individuals that are critical of their operations but those who would improve them.

This question is more applicable to those being interviewed for supervisory or managerial roles. Your answer should be based on what your *research* revealed about the needs of the organization or the department with which you are being interviewed.

You must understand the requirements of the role and develop a plan while preparing for the interview that shows a good understanding of the areas of need there, which you will validate within the first week or month of employment. The point is that you should have a clear objective of what to focus on and how to go about achieving that objective; a combination of your strategy and activity plans is what the panel wants to hear.

Primarily, the panel may not be assessing how correct your answers are as much as your ability to think creatively and demonstrate that you understand the possible gaps in their operation.

In your answer to this question, the panel expects to hear how you intend to make a difference within a short time, such as in the first 100 days. It is usually advisable that you focus on one or two major areas.

Make what you will focus on clear to the panel without losing sight of other key performance areas. For example, one being interviewed for a sales manager position in a company that has not maximized the potentials in key market sectors could say:

> *"Within the first quarter of employment, I plan to structure the corporate sales team to focus on key industry sectors rather than geographical territories and concentrate the attention of my team on the top two industries in the economy, namely, telecommunications and agriculture. I have learned from experience that a large proportion of revenues in sales comes from a few customers, so my team will focus on those few top customers without losing sight of average customers."*

Then you can mention the number of personnel you will deploy to focus on each of the industries mentioned above, and so on. This shows you are thinking and planning ahead.

Please see appendix C page 107 for your relevant exercise.

### 6. Tell us about your current job or responsibilities.

When you are asked questions relating to your current or previous positions, it's important to be specific and to be positive about what you are doing or what you did in your previous position(s).

The best way to respond is to describe your responsibilities in detail and to connect them to the job for which you are being interviewed. Try to tie your responsibilities to those listed in the job description for the new position so the interviewer will see that you have the qualifications and experience necessary to do the job. Focus on the three to five responsibilities that are directly related to the new job's requirements, and mention what your key achievements have been for each of the responsibilities mentioned.

For example, an applicant for a sales position might say:

> "I was responsible for increasing the sales of our products to retail shops, and over the last two years I achieved a 100 percent growth in sales turnover and increased our retail distribution by 50 percent."

A prospective production officer could answer:

> "As a production officer, I was responsible for the design and development of our activity schedule, which has helped the factory to minimize the downtime for our machines, and staff reporting late to the plant has become a thing of the past. It may interest you to know how we achieved that."

Then the applicant would explain briefly how he or she did it and conclude by saying:

> "The bottom line is that we doubled our output in just six months."

**You don't impress with your responsibilities or job description; you impress with your results and achievements.**

Please see appendix C page 108 for your relevant exercise.

## 7. What is your greatest weakness?

When you're asked for your greatest weakness, you can turn this seemingly negative question into a positive one. For example, you might say:

- *"Being organized wasn't my strongest point, but I have implemented a time management system that really helped my organization skills."*

- *"I used to wait until the last minute to set appointments for the coming week, but I realized that scheduling in advance makes much more sense."*

- *"I like to make sure that my work is perfect, so I tend to spend a little too much time checking it. However, I've come to a good balance by setting up a system to ensure everything is done correctly the first time."*

Instead of belaboring your weaknesses, let the panel ask any follow-up questions, such as, "What is that system?"

Don't fall into the trap of saying you don't have a weakness, which is what I hear many people say a lot of times. At the same time, don't reinforce that you have a weakness.

**Observe in the examples above that we have deliberately avoided use of the word "weakness."**

Please see appendix C page 109 for your relevant exercise.

## 8. What are your strengths?

When you are asked about your strengths, it's important to discuss attributes that will qualify you for the job. For example, your football-juggling artistry has nothing to do with getting an insurance job. The best way to respond to this question is to describe the skills and experience that relate to the job for which you have applied. For example, you might say:

- *"When I'm working on a project, I don't want to just meet deadlines but prefer to complete the project well ahead of schedule, which has always made my managers look good."*

- *"I have exceeded my sales goals every quarter and have earned a bonus each year since I started with my current employer."*

- *"My time management skills are excellent, and I'm organized, efficient, and take pride in excelling at my work."*

- *"I have great communication skills and can work with different types of people of varying personalities and skill levels. I am motivated, disciplined, and focused and I am determined to get my job done well."*

- *"I have a solid background in accounts receivables and great problem-solving abilities, and I get things done with little supervision."*

Please see appendix C page 109 for your relevant exercise.

## 9. Why did you leave your job, or why do you want to leave your job?

This is by far the most important question asked by experienced interviewers and the answers you provide here may be what determine if you get hired.

Jack Welch, in his book *Winning* said of this question, "If I had just one area to probe in an interview, it would be about why the candidate left his previous job, and the one before that."

He says that there is so much information in the answers the candidate provides. Whether it was the environment, the boss or the team, whatever made him or her leave tells more about him or her than any other piece of data.

This is the reason most interviewers would listen closely and try to get in the candidate's skin. And for this reason you should answer this question thoughtfully and professionally in a manner that shows you are the person for the job.

This question could also be a trap when you attend interviews. Never run down your present or previous employers. Doing so does not show good character but tells your prospective employer that you may be difficult to please and may run them down if you have an opportunity. Find a way to speak well of your current employer even when it's hard to do so.

When asked such questions, answer positively by focusing on reasons that pull you to the prospective employer rather than on those that are sending you away from the current one.

The reason for wanting to join a company could be anything from the desire for greater challenges, the work environment to the dynamic management team. Other reasons for desiring to join a company are discussed under the question, *why do you want to work for us?*

However, in certain instances, your reason may include a shortcoming of your present or most recent position. In these cases, be brief, straight to the point, and as honest as you can without hurting yourself. For example, you might say:

- *"There isn't room for growth with my current employer and I'm ready to move on to a new and bigger challenge to grow my career, and I believe this is my opportunity."*
- *"I am seeking a position with a stable company that has room for growth and opportunity for advancement."*
- *"I was laid off from my last position when our department was eliminated during corporate restructuring."*

Remember that most employers will run a check on your references, especially your previous employer; so tell the truth in the best way possible.

Usually when people have been shown the door (fired), they become defensive and depressed. Consider the following sample forthright response given by an executive who was once fired from his job:

> *"Listen, I messed up,"* he said. *"My boss and I had agreed to clear-cut objectives and I missed them. I waited too long to let go of two direct reports who weren't delivering. I didn't cut down costs fast enough when the downturn was approaching. I was just too*

*optimistic."* He then added, *"I'm determined to be more externally focused from now on, and I will definitely move faster on underperforming people. One of my objectives is to prove I don't make the same mistakes twice."*

If you have been shown the door, you need to project realism, levelheadedness, and optimism. You need to draw from your reservoir of confidence. Say what happened, say what you have learned, and never be afraid to ask, *"Just give me a chance."* Definitely some will.

Please see appendix C page 110 for your relevant exercise.

**10. Why do you want to work for us?**

This typical interview question is usually asked to find out whether you are sufficiently interested in the job to have learned something about the company. The best way to answer this question is to be prepared and be knowledgeable about the company.

Here, and throughout the interview, a good answer comes from having done your homework so you can speak in terms of the company's needs. You might say that your research has shown that the company is doing things you are passionate about, and that it's doing them in ways that deeply interest you. For example, if the organization is known for strong management, your answer should mention that you would like to be a part of such a team.

If the company places emphasis on extensive product distribution, emphasize that you like exploring new markets, that you are a hands-on salesperson, and that you know this is a place where aggressive sales and distribution are encouraged. If the company lays emphasis on research and development, stress that you are passionate about creating new things. If the organization stresses financial controls, your answer should mention an interest in and value for numbers.

Remember that the reason for applying to a company could be anything from the desire for greater challenges, fulfillment of a personal vision or goal, reputation of the prospective company in the market place, to their quality goods and services. Select the one that applies in your case, and add relevant details about the company to show that it can help you address those reasons.

If you feel that you have to concoct an answer to this question—for example, the company stresses research or product distribution, which doesn't really interest you—then you probably should not be taking that interview because you are probably not suited for a job with that organization. Your homework should include learning enough about the company to avoid places where you wouldn't be able to function at your best.

**It's difficult to con an interviewer, but even if you should succeed at it, your prize is a job you don't really want and at which you may perform poorly.**

Please see appendix C page 110 for your relevant exercise.

**11. How much do you want to earn?**

Whenever possible, say as little as you can about the salary until you reach the "final" stage of the interview process. At that point, you know that the company is genuinely interested in you and that it is likely to be flexible in salary negotiations.

Don't sell yourself short, but continue to stress that the job itself is the most important thing on your mind. The interviewer may be trying to determine just how much you want the job, but don't give the impression that money is all that is important to you.

Link questions of salary to the work itself. Before you start salary negotiations with a prospective employer, find out how much the job is worth. If you've worked in the industry, you probably have a good idea already. If not, take the time to research salaries in the industry so you are prepared to negotiate for what you're worth: a fair salary and a job that's rewarding and exciting.

Do your best not to bring up compensation until the employer makes you an offer. If you're asked what your salary requirements are, say that they are open based upon the position and the overall compensation package, especially if you are earning much less than what the job you are being interviewed is likely to offer. Tell the employer you'd like to know more about the responsibilities and the challenges of the job prior to discussing salary. You might be able to get the interviewer to tell you the salary range for the position so you can explain where you think your experience places you in that range. Another option is to give the employer a salary range based on the salary research you've done. If the job is in another location, remember to factor in cost-of-living expenses.

*The Different Ways to Handle an Offer*
Once you receive an offer, you may not want to accept or reject it right away. A simple *"I need to think it over"* or counteroffer may get you an increase on the original offer. If you're undecided about the position, a straightforward "no" may also bring you a better offer—or it may result in the offer being withdrawn.

If you are pressed to mention a figure, be careful not to mention an unrealistic one. For instance, if you currently earn $2,000 per month at a similar job, it is unrealistic to ask for a salary of $7,000 per month unless you are being grossly underpaid by your current employer.

Assuming you are moving into a job in a field in which you have experience, a 25-50 percent increase in pay is reasonable. You can push for 100 percent over what you currently earn if, based on industry standards for your role, you are being underpaid or you are being interviewed for a higher position with more responsibilities. A 200-300 percent increase over what you earn may indicate that you are greedy, unreasonable, or both and cause the employer to rethink his or her decision to offer you employment. In any case, if you convince the panel you are the person they have been seeking, they are likely to pay you what is commensurate with the position. Your job is to get them to agree to a salary as high in their acceptable salary range as possible.

*Don't Shortchange Yourself in the Negotiation*
In the circumstance that the prospective employer insists on you stating your minimum acceptable offer, it is important for you to have thought about the minimum acceptable amount that makes the job worth your while.

The remuneration may not be your primary consideration, but you should not shortchange yourself; know your worth, ask for it, and you will get it! Ask for what you deserve. The job should be both professionally challenging and financially rewarding.

Please see appendix C page 111 for your relevant exercise.

**12. What motivates you?**

There is no right or wrong answer to this question. The interviewer is trying to understand the key to your being successful in the job for which you are being interviewed and wants to make sure it is a good fit. In advance of your interview, consider what motivates you and come up with some specific examples to share. For example, you could say:

- *"I was responsible for several projects in which I directed key implementation processes. The teams achieved 100 percent on-time delivery of our turnkey sites. I was motivated both by the challenge of finishing the projects ahead of schedule and by managing the teams that achieved our goals."*

- *"I have always wanted to ensure that my company's clients get the best customer service I can provide. I've always felt that it's important, both to me personally and for the company, to provide a positive customer experience. I am always delighted when customers walk out of my service center with a smile!"*

Please see appendix C page 111 for your relevant exercise.

## 13. When can you start?

Never say you can start right away unless you are currently unemployed. Display good professionalism by facilitating a proper transition of your responsibilities in your current job before starting a new one. Doing so shows your new employer that you are thorough and that when it is time to move again, you will not leave them without notice.

Your answer ultimately depends on your current employment contract and the amount of notice it stipulates that you must give your employer. Most employers are willing to wait a few weeks or months to get the best candidate.

You could say:

> *"My current employment contract stipulates that I give one month notice. Plus that I'm leading a project team and would need time to properly handover to the person who would succeed me on the project . . . (mention the date) is the most suitable date to resume."*

Please see appendix C page 112 for your relevant exercise.

## 14. Your resume is not very impressive! Why should we employ you?

This is my advice—don't oversell yourself. There's nothing less appealing than an applicant with a wishy-washy record overselling himself with lots of bravado. Experienced managers can spot the fakery from a distance. Jack Welch suggests a good answer:

> *"I know my grades aren't that great. I spent a lot of time playing intramural sports and to be honest, a lot of time with my friends. I definitely could have studied more, but I had other priorities, which probably weren't the best ones. The reason you should still hire me is because I never give up on a challenge, I work hard, I believe in your product and I admire your company and I know I can contribute here."*

Please see appendix C page 112 for your relevant exercise.

**15. Do you have any questions for us?**

When they finish questioning you, the interviewers will probably ask if you have any questions, so you should have some ready. Ask questions that will help you learn more about the employer and will let the interviewer know you are interested in working there. Use what you learned about the company through your research as a starting point.

A key consideration in asking a good question is to ensure that the panel is not embarrassed by your question and that you don't look like you are poorly prepared. Your questions must show that you are thinking. Don't ask about salary, benefits, or vacations, as those all imply, "What will you do for me?" Keep your questions brief and sharp. Here are some good questions to ask:

- *"What is a typical career path in your organization for someone with my skills and experience?"*

- *"How has the current economic situation affected your advertising spending or your new product development activities?"*

- *"What do you like about working here?"*

- *"Who does this position report to, and what is management's disposition to training and skill acquisition for staff?"*

Please see appendix C page 112 for your relevant exercise.

For more practice questions and answers please visit www.harrynnoli.com

# PART IV
## THE OFFER AND CHOICES

CHAPTER **8**

# After the Job Interview

*Choice, not chance, determines human destiny.*

Robert W. Ellis

## Post-interview Follow-up

Within 24 hours of going for a job interview, send a thank-you note through the mail or email (as long as you've communicated with the recipient through email before, as otherwise your note may end up in the recipient's spam folder) to follow up. This is your chance to reiterate something you mentioned on the interview or bring up something you forgot to mention. It is also a courtesy to thank your interviewers for taking their valuable time to consider you for employment.

You can send a note to each person who took part in your interview. If you don't remember the name of each person, call human resources for some help. Keep your note brief. Sending a thank-you note sets you apart from those who forgot to or chose not to do so.

Generally, while this is not mandatory, following up can help you rise above the crowd and can reinforce your candidature to the hiring manager. It conveys passion for the job, which every hiring manager looks out for. Not following up could even cost you the job especially in a situation where a number of candidates did exceptionally well. A professional survey reported that 15% of hiring managers wouldn't hire someone who didn't send a note, and 32% would think less of them.

Waiting to hear from a potential employer after a job interview can be torturous. If the prospective employer told you when you could expect to hear from them, wait a week or two after that date before calling them. However, rather than being concerned about calling especially when the interviewer didn't expressly say so, be focused on your next interview.

**Interview Follow-up Tips**

Its advisable to take the time to follow up with everyone you met and review the tips below on how to follow-up after an interview:

1. Follow up after both in-person and phone interviews.

2. Send personal thank you email to everyone you met with.

3. Email is one of the fastest ways to say thank you. A well constructed thank you message from your mobile phone should suffice.

4. Send your email message as soon as possible after the interview.

5. Consider sending a handwritten thank you note as well.

6. Send your note within 24 hours of the interview.

7. Use this opportunity to reiterate your interest in the job and the company. Let your passion show.

8. Highlight your relevant skills.

9. Mention anything you forgot to say during the interview.

10. Keep your correspondence short and simple.

11. Pay attention to the details; you cant afford any grammatical or syntax errors.

12. Proofread your email and notes before you send them.

## Selecting the Right Job for You

Selecting the right job for you could be as challenging as finding one in the first place where there are lots of candidates competing for same job. In this section of the book I will attempt to suggest some signals to look out for in finding the right job. When you find the kind of job with these signals or indicators, you will enjoy it so much it wouldn't feel like work anymore!

Here are some signals or indicators to look out for.

**1. The People**

Everything else can be perfect about a job—the role, the remuneration, the location, and the opportunities—but if you do not enjoy the company of your colleagues on a day-to-day basis, work can be frustrating. It is important to work in an environment where you enjoy the company of others because that is where you will spend most of your time.

It is a good pointer if you find that the people in the company that has made you an offer or that you recently joined are just like you! In the sense that you can relate with them and genuinely enjoy their company. It is not unusual to find people who have taken jobs in companies where they do not share the corporate ideology, values (both written and unwritten), and culture. These obviously will affect how free they are, how well they handle criticisms and confrontational issues, how they relate and interact at meetings etc. If these don't fit with your personal values then you are constrained to put on a false impression to get along with the team everyday, and what a miserable work experience you would have. Avoid such jobs and if you find you are already in it, get out as soon as possible. Go and find your kind of people. The story below is a typical scenario.

John changed his job from a fast moving consumer goods company (FMCG) to a telecommunications company. Everything seemed right: the pay, the position, and the seeming opportunity for growth. The problem was, the people's culture, system and values within the organization were disjointed; organization was poor with little empathy, people functioned in small informal clusters more on emotional rather than professional basis. He knew he didn't fit in but had to stay on because the options in the market were limited at the time. He earned far beyond economic average by virtue of the industry he joined. The result of this was he never really performed at his peak and was not promoted for about seven years that he worked in the organization. He however got another job offer in a top-flight international organization with a better work environment and before long he rose to become the chief executive.

In retrospect, the move from the FMCG was neither fulfilling nor rewarding because of the "people."

Find the company with the right kind of people early in your career. The earlier you do, the better. Even if a job appears ideal in every aspect, without shared values and ideology it's not ideal for you.

## 2. Growth Opportunity

Another indicator of a good job-fit is the opportunity to grow and learn. Always consider the prospects you have in the job you are about to take or have resumed.

Go for the job that feels like a stretch not a stroll. You should feel that you can handle most of the work but at the same time you should also feel that there are skills and knowledge you need on the job that you don't have. The job should make you think, "I am going to learn something new here." Don't jump on a job simply because the pay is good and it looks like a "stroll in the park" for you, choose the job that will challenge your energy, skills and ability. Reconsider taking the job where you feel you are the expert and smartest person; "a superstar."

It is advisable to take up a job that is challenging because it helps you learn and grow. However, the tendency to mess up things is there when you take up such a challenging job. That is why you should make sure to join a company where learning is treasured, growth for every employee is a real objective, and mistakes are treated as a learning experience. Also make sure there are people in the organization you can reach out to for coaching and mentoring.

A young graduate called Teddy (not real name) fresh from the university landed a dream job in a big organization and over a five-year period rose to become a director when his other colleagues were yet to be promoted into managerial positions. His "fortune" was more as a result of unusually favorable circumstances than hard work, even though he was hard working. But others were just as hard working as he was. In his case, he was promoted into the position that was clearly bigger than what his level of competence at the time could handle.

In his words, "I was scared and apprehensive at first with no idea of what a human resources director was supposed to be doing; I was barely 5 years on the job." However, within a few months, Teddy, had learnt enough new skills on human management and leadership to start excelling on the job.

Looking back after the first year he said, "It was a tough call, I entered many meetings with my subordinates—many of whom were more experienced than I—feeling jittery but I tried hard to conceal all that! Its all fun now, I have settled in." He has been on the job for over six years now and doing well.

Early in career pursuit for most people, they find jobs they are most suited for which may not be stretching in any way. However, if you find yourself with a job that appears too big at the beginning don't be afraid. If you are good enough to be hired or promoted as in the case of Teddy, be rest assured you'll grow into it, and be better for the experience.

## 3. Brand and Industry Leverage

When you work for an organization that has a strong brand equity, the value it confers on your resume most times goes beyond the roles you performed while you were there. Such jobs help you when you leave.

Jack Welch says, "Working for some companies is like winning an Olympic medal. For the rest of your career you are associated with great performance and success." When sifting through resumes most interviewers would prioritize candidates with experience from big and reputable corporate organizations—those with enormous "employee brand."

Companies with good employee brand are those whose people get a real credential by working there for a few years. Strong brands like Apple, Microsoft, GlaxoSmithKline, GE etc., have enormous employee brand; having them in your resume is great value.

But this alone should not determine your job decisions, so that you don't end up in a highly respected company that has a terrible work environment, difficult bosses and offers limited responsibilities. Although these may not be so common with the caliber of companies we're referring to.

Smaller organizations may not have strong employee brand but could offer you experiences and exposure that you ordinarily may not get from the bigger organizations. You get a chance to manage people earlier in your career, run projects, departments, and work more closely with the management team and the board. This would count for you in both small and big organizations. Some good companies with high employee brand do seek candidates with such exposures.

A company can influence your future prospects positively or negatively either because of their reputation as discussed above or because of their industry. At different times we've had booms, and crises in different industries. Its important to know where the industry you are joining is headed. A former air force officer now a business executive captured this well. He said:

> "When I was on a mission, I would always ask, 'What is our altitude? What are the weather conditions ahead? Where is the enemy?' He says:

> "It's same in business, you need to know same about your job or industry. Are you getting yourself into a turnaround situation? Are the economics fatal? How tough is competition? Has the industry peaked, or is it just getting off the ground? Are the results expected from me reasonable or am I walking into a trap?"

Ask these questions and you may be surprised that the company you like has a bleak future. Consider the boom of the energy crises in the '70s with the attendant rise in the need of geologists by companies engaged in upstream oil and gas business, the boom of the high technology and finance industries in the '80s and '90s, the boom of mobile telecommunications from late '90s to late 2000s, the burst of the finance industry globally in the late 2000s, which led to the current global recession. About the same time there was a rise in usage of social media.

We can go on and on. It is your responsibility to know where your industry is headed and ensure to ride the crest. Avoid shrinking markets!

## 4. Follow your Passion

Many live their lives for others and their choices including the types of jobs they take up are dependent on the opinion of these key influencers who could be parents, spouses, teachers, friends, or classmates. The earlier you come to terms in your career with the consequences of this action the better for you. Be sure of this, working to fulfill someone else's dream has dare consequences and it is advisable to avoid this pitfall.

I heard a story recently, of a middle age medical doctor in the Bahamas who had practiced medicine for 22 years and finally broke down after he had come to terms with "reality" because in his words:

> "I hate medicine and these 22 years I lived a lie, I only studied medicine because my father wanted me to, but all the while I wanted to paint. Everyday after my rounds in the hospital I retired into my passion, which is painting."

He eventually gave up his successful medical practice, handed it over to competent doctors and focused on his passion. In the very first exhibition he held, where he showcased all his paintings of over two decades, he made more money than in all his 22 years of medical practice. Today he runs a successful art gallery and makes a fortune selling paintings. How about that for a medical doctor with 22 years experience!

Follow your passion and not the dreams of others for you.

I also learnt of someone who became a doctor because his entire childhood, his mother always introduced him to friends and acquaintances by saying, "And he's my doctor!" He didn't hate the profession I gathered, but you've never met anyone more eager to retire.

Very few people have the total freedom to take a job just for themselves. In some instances people take jobs because their spouses want them to travel less or to be in a particular location and therefore might lose out on a promotion. Others take up jobs to enable them remain in certain cities they believe offer them opportunities, whether real or imagined. Many especially in the less developed economies would rather remain at urban areas because of the notion that they can't be successful except they work in the cities, whereas greater opportunities may lie in the suburb or rural communities.

Over the course of your career, your passion will surely call you at one point or another. If you choose to go, that's great—because therein lies your opportunity for unlimited success—if you choose not to go, be convinced about the reason for your choice and live with it.

## 5. Genuine Love for the Work

This may hold the key to success in your career.

While we seek jobs that are professionally fulfilling and financially rewarding, to become exceptional in your chosen field or career you must find that job that excites you and apply yourself to it.

Raymond Albert "Ray" Kroc, founder of McDonald's in his several sessions with young professionals would tell them that the first thing a business executive needs is the love of an idea. He says:

> "Don't go for the money, otherwise you'll be working for money all your life!"

Loving your work is particularly important if you are a young person. If you want to grow up to self-actualization (reaching your highest potential), you must apply yourself to what you love and ought to be doing.

Every job has rough periods and there will be times when you work mainly to make ends meet. But in the best job scenario, you love the work; at least something about the job should excite you and tug at your heart. This could be anything from the sales meeting, the national sales conference, the Town Hall meetings, the fun times with colleagues at the workstations to the challenges on the job itself. Something should turn you on otherwise you wont find any meaning or fulfillment on the job. If the job doesn't excite you, don't settle for it.

The good news is, it's not hard to find a job that touches your core; every piece of work has the potential since the important thing is the way you feel about it deep inside. If you feel good about it you will want to put in your best and consequently you get better at it at a faster rate.

And when you become better you will eventually attract the best pay in the industry as you command greater respect as an expert in your career with the attendant satisfaction of accomplishment.

# Conclusion

*If money is your hope for independence you will never have it. The only real security that a man will have in this world is a reserve of knowledge, experience, and ability.*

Henry Ford I

Remember that the only way to secure the job is to first become someone who can add value to the organization. Whenever I have the opportunity to interview people for jobs, I always look for candidates who have something to offer, who want to help me solve problems in the office.

**Work with the Company, Not for the Company**
Until you can demonstrate to your prospective employer that you are the solution he or she is looking for, you are likely to remain an applicant, not an employee.

You can start out now; as a prospecting employee, be clear on how you can add value to the need of a prospective employer. You can either work for a company to achieve your own goals or work with a company, pursuing its goals as your own. Most people want to work for companies, but smart professionals would rather work with them.

Consider the story of Edwin C. Barnes, whose desire was definite: he wanted to work with the great inventor, Thomas Edison, not for him.

He didn't know Edison personally or have enough money to pay his railroad fare to Orange, New Jersey, where Edison's company was situated.

When he finally got to Orange, Barnes did not say to himself, "I will try to induce Edison to give me a job of some sort." He said, "I will see Edison and put him on notice that I have come to go into business with him."

He did not say, "I will work there for a few months, and if I get no encouragement, I will quit and get a job somewhere else." He did say, "I will start anywhere. I will do anything Edison tells me to do, but before I am through, I will be his associate."

He did not say, "I will keep my eyes open for another opportunity in case I fail to get what I want in the Edison organization." He did say, "There is but one thing in this world that I am determined to have, and that is a business association with Thomas Edison. I will burn all bridges behind me and stake my entire future on my ability to get what I want."

A few years after he started work as a floor cleaner with Edison, his break came and he became a multimillionaire salesman who helped thousands of people benefit from Edison's dictation machines. He was so good at selling the machines that it led to the slogan, "Made by Edison, sold by Barnes."

## 7 Key Elements of Success
Many factors, tangible and intangible, were responsible for transforming Edwin Barnes from a poor, young floor-cleaner to one of the most successful and capable salesmen Edison ever knew. His

success can be attributed to traits that I strongly recommend to young professionals and anyone who wants to be successful in life. These traits made Edwin Barnes see the potential of the dictation machines and Edison's other inventions when others doubted whether the inventions could be commercially successful:

1. He knew exactly what he wanted to accomplish.

2. He was willing to start at the bottom in order to gain expertise and exposure.

3. He had dogged determination to bring his goals to reality.

4. He created and seized opportunities.

5. In alignment with his goals, he found a way to help other people become more successful.

6. He made himself invaluable at his work.

7. He was committed to providing customers with excellent service.

For more on the traits that led to the remarkable success that Barnes enjoyed, refer to my book, *Grow Rich, the Secrets of the Rich*.

Correct application of knowledge is what gives you the edge in every human endeavor; every prospective employer has a problem that they are trying to solve and for which they are conducting the interview you are attending. No company employs staff because things are fine; they employ staff because there are gaps or problems in the organizations that the suitable candidate can help to fill or solve.

With this in mind, approach every interview as a solution-provider, not a job seeker. When you secure the job, work to the top using Edwin Barnes' traits.

We have discussed the "3R" strategy, the 5-SPA to deploy in securing your dream job, and answers to typical interview questions, all of which will assist you in building the career of your dreams.

**Assess Your Market Value**
Here is my advice to corporate executives: it is a virtue to have staying power on a job, especially when doing so is in line with your long-term career plan. Exceptions to this position are when your professional and career interests are not served by remaining on the job, and if there is no alignment of values and ideology. As much as possible employees should stay focused and build their careers with their respective organizations. If your skills and talents are well aligned with your job and your employer, you can become a true partner with your organization and live the Edwin Barnes' experience.

Even when your career interests are not served, put in your best on the job while you are there, because every knowledge or skill gained doing something worthwhile adds to your value. Remember, all that glitters is not gold—the new job in some instances may not in reality be better than the current one. Weigh your options well before making a career or job decision.

However, if your professional and career interests are not served, and you are not making good progress on the job as a result of this, don't feel hemmed in or trapped. If after an objective appraisal a job change seems a reasonable solution, then pursue it.

There may be instances where an employer may mistake staff loyalty for lack of ability and marketability; therefore, it may not out of place to explore new opportunities by occasionally attending interviews. If you are successful at the interview and get an offer, you could use this as a tool to negotiate a better deal with your employer, but don't give them an ultimatum!

There are instances where people who have found themselves in job situations that didn't serve their career or long-term interests have stepped aside from their jobs and taken up new jobs to refresh themselves. Some of such people returned to their former companies when the conditions improved and where offered more challenging responsibilities. For this, it is important to treat your former employers well, and with respect.

**You're Worth More**
Know this, you are worth more than any employer can make you feel. Always pursue your best value, and one of the ways to do this is to do an excellent work in the job you currently have, and demand your fair compensation based on demonstrable value you have added to the organization. As mentioned earlier, you could explore other opportunities but your ultimate best value is to gain sufficient experience with your employer then launch out and do something worthwhile with your skills, which will impact positively on your environment.

Frequent change in jobs may be an indication of instability in an individual. As much as possible stay with your current employer, value what you have and make a difference with them. But don't stay on a job out of fear or a false sense of security because no job can offer you the desired security and none owes you one! The best job security is to find something you are good at and to work on perfecting your skills at doing it.

If you cannot find a company that will employ you, don't be discouraged, make a job; start something. Look around you; the problems in your environment are your opportunity! Ask yourself what you are good at that is constructive for society and take some actions in that direction at once.

There are many vocations you can begin without financial capital, so don't consider financial limitation as an excuse for failing to start. If you articulate your dream, break it down to simple goals, and plan how to achieve them, soon someone with the required finances will come along! Remember that there are many types of capital, only one of which (and probably not the most important) is financial capital. Your mental capital—the ideas you can come up with—is the most important capital, and your social capital is invaluable, as it has been rightly said that your network (those in your social circle) is your net worth.

Apply your mind and come up with creative ideas to solving the problem. True success lies in identifying a need or a demand and meeting it with a solution you can offer to the market.

See you at the top!

# Appendix A

# SWOT Analysis

Map your Strengths, Weaknesses, Opportunities and Threats with those of the organization.

|  | Internal | | External | |
|---|---|---|---|---|
|  | Strength | Weaknesses | Opportunities | Threats |
| Organization | 1.<br>2.<br>3.<br>4. | 1.<br>2.<br>3. | 1.<br>2.<br>3.<br>4. | 1.<br>2.<br>3. |
| Self | 1.<br>2.<br>3.<br>4. | 1.<br>2.<br>3. | 1.<br>2.<br>3.<br>4. | 1.<br>2.<br>3. |

# Appendix B

# Your 5-Star Points Approach

Worksheet 1 (Your answers may differ for each interview.)

What are your 5-SPA? List them:

Achievements, academic:

1. _____
   _____
   _____

2. _____
   _____
   _____

3. _____
   _____
   _____

Achievements, professional:

1. _____
   _____
   _____

2. _____
   _____
   _____

3. _____
   _____
   _____

I speak the following languages:

1. _____
2. _____
3. _____

I am experienced in the following areas that are vital to the job for which I'm being interviewed. (Indicate years of experience in each role.)

1. _____
   _____
   _____

2. _____
   _____
   _____

3. _____
   _____
   _____

I have specialized knowledge of the terrain and market as follows. Indicate how the specialized knowledge relates to the job.

1. _____
   _____
   _____

2. _____
   _____
   _____

3. _____
   _____
   _____

My attitude and disposition in life that make me the best candidate for the job:

1. _____
   _____
   _____

2. _____
   _____
   _____

3. _____
   _____
   _____

List other Star Points. (Consider all other strong points that qualify you for the job.)

1. _____
   _____
   _____

2. _____
   _____
   _____

3. _____
   _____
   _____

# Appendix C

# Your Answers to Typical Interview Questions

Worksheet 2 (Your answers may differ for each interview.)

**1. Tell us about yourself.**

(Write the answer exactly as you would like to say it during the interview. Don't assume you will say the right thing at the interview, but practice and rehearse it here first, whether you are adopting the Story Style or Punch Line Method. Time yourself to ensure your answer takes no more than three minutes.)

_____
_____
_____
_____
_____
_____
_____
_____

**2. Why should we employ you?**

(Consider what the qualities of the ideal person for that position should be and relate them to your skills and accomplishments. List the accomplishments that show that you are the best person for the job.)

1. _____

2. _____

3. _____

4. _____

5. _____

**3. What work experience do you have?**

(List your work experiences related to the job, including summer jobs and national service assignments for fresh graduates and young professionals.)

1. _____
   _____
   _____
   _____

2. _____
   _____
   _____
   _____

3. _____
   _____
   _____
   _____

**4. What are your goals for the future, or where do you see yourself in five to seven years?**

(Make your response relevant to the position and the company with which you are interviewing. You could start by saying, "In a firm like yours, I would like to . . .")_____
_____
_____
_____
_____

_____
_____
_____
_____
_____
_____
_____
_____
_____
_____
_____."

**5. If we employ you, what would you do differently from what the company currently does? In other words are there changes you would make to enhance the performance of the organization or department?**

_____

(What key objectives will you seek to achieve in the first 3-6 months and how)

1. _____
_____
_____
_____

2. _____
_____
_____
_____

## 6. Tell us about your current job/ responsibilities

(List a few roles you have played and your key achievements in a way that connects to the job for which you are being interviewed.)

1. Role 1 _____
   _____

   Achievement(s): _____
   _____
   _____
   _____

2. Role 1 _____
   _____

   Achievement(s): _____
   _____
   _____
   _____

3. Role 1 _____
   _____

   Achievement(s): _____
   _____
   _____
   _____

4. Role 1 _____
   _____

   Achievement(s): _____
   _____

5. Role 1 _____

   Achievement(s): _____
   _____
   _____
   _____

Note that you are likely to have more than five key roles or responsibilities, in practice however, mentioning three key roles with your major achievements would suffice.

### 7. What is your greatest weakness?

(Avoid using the word "weakness," but show how you have worked to correct your weakness.)

_____
_____
_____
_____

### 8. What are your strengths?

(Describe the skills and experiences that relate to the job for which you are applying.)

1. _____
   _____
   _____
   _____

2. _____
   _____
   _____
   _____

**9. Why did you leave your job, or why do you want to leave your job?**

(Always tell the truth, but don't complain.)

1. _____
   _____
   _____
   _____

2. _____
   _____
   _____
   _____

**10. Why do you want to work for us?**

(Here is where your research is important. What do you like about the company?)

1. _____
   _____
   _____
   _____

2. _____
_____
_____
_____

3. _____
_____
_____
_____

## 11. How much do you want to earn?

Decide your range:

Your desired pay based on your market value/industry standards:
_____

The minimum level acceptable: _____
_____

## 12. What motivates you?

(Consider the job you are interviewing for and write what motivates you.)

_____
_____
_____
_____

**13. When can you start?**

(Never say you can start right away unless you are currently unemployed. Be clear about the terms for resignation in your current employment.)

_____
_____
_____
_____

**14. Your resume is not very impressive! Why should we employ you?**

_____
_____
_____
_____

**15. Do you have any questions for us?**

(Ask about the company and the job; don't ask about salary, benefits, or vacations. Two questions are sufficient.)

1. _____
_____
_____
_____

2. _____
   _____
   _____
   _____

For more practice questions and answers please visit www.harrynnoli.com

# Appendix D

# Types of Job Interviews

## The Screening Interview

Your first interview with an employer will often be the Screening Interview, usually with someone in human resources. It may take place in person or over the telephone. The interviewer will have a copy of your resume and will try to verify the information on it and determine whether you meet the minimum qualifications for the job. If you do, he or she will pass you on to the next step. The employer could also require you to take a test to determine your aptitude during the screening stage.

## Phone Interview

Employers use Phone Interviews as one of the ways to identify, qualify, and recruit candidates for employment. They are often used to screen candidates in order to narrow the pool of applicants who will be invited for in-person interviews. The advantages of this type of interviews are that they help to reduce cost expended in interviewing out-of-town candidates and quicken the recruitment process.

It's important that you are prepared while searching for a job for a possible phone interview at a short notice. Usually a recruiter would call and ask if you have a few moments to talk. Most times the recruiter is willing to reschedule to a time suitable for you.

It's important that you prepare for a phone interview just as you would for a regular interview. Speak audibly, clearly and slowly to make the right impact, because you don't have the benefit of a visual or personal component associated with in-person interviews.

Revise the entire typical job interview questions discussed in this book and the suggested answers. For more exercise questions and answers please visit www.harrynnoli.com

*During the Phone Interview*

1. Smile. Smiling will project a warm and positive image to the listener and will change the tone of your voice.

2. Do keep a glass of water handy, in case you need a sip.

3. Don't chew gum, smoke eat, or drink.

*Seven Key Points to Note During a Phone Interview*

1. Keep your CV or resume within reach for quick reference. As much as possible know your resume by heart, especially roles currently performed and key accomplishments with dates.

2. Have a pen and paper handy or an electronic device for note taking.

3. Turn call-waiting off if using a cell phone so your call isn't interrupted.

4. If the time isn't convenient, ask if you could talk at another time and suggest some alternatives.

5. Clear the room—kids and the pets may distract, therefore; let them stay out for the duration of the interview. Turn off the sound and the TV sets, and any other thing that may distract you. Close the door.

6. If you share an office with colleagues excuse yourself from the office and find a suitable place where you would not be interrupted.

7. It is preferable to use a landline rather than your cell phone to avoid network related problems like dropped call or cell phone static on the line.

**The Selection Interview**

The Selection Interview is the step in the process of hiring, which makes people the most anxious. The employer knows you are qualified to do the job but needs to know whether you have the personality necessary to "fit in." Someone who can't interact well with management and co-workers may disrupt the operations of an entire department or organization and ultimately affect the company's bottom line. Many experts feel that a prospective employee's "fit" can be determined within the first several minutes of the interview.

Since more than one person being interviewed for a single opening may appear to fit in, job candidates are often invited back for several interviews with a variety of people before a final choice is made.

## The Group Interview
In the Group Interview, which tends to be most applicable for operational level positions, several job candidates are questioned at the same time. The interviewer(s) may give the group a topic to discuss or a simple project or game to perform while the interviewers watch directly or remotely. Additional details were provided in the main text of this book.

## The Panel Interview
A Panel Interview is the reverse of a group interview, as several people interview a single candidate at once. Although a panel interview can be intimidating, it is an opportunity to impress several people at once with your personality, ability, and qualifications. Additional details about the panel interview were provided in the main text of this book.

## The Stress Interview
The Stress Interview is a technique employers sometimes use to weed out candidates who cannot handle adversity. In this type of interview, the interviewer tries to introduce stress into the interview by asking questions so quickly that the candidate doesn't have time to answer each one or by responding to a candidate's answers with silence. The interviewer may also ask odd questions, pretend not to hear the candidate's answers but observe how he or she responds to the unusual questions. In some stress interviews, candidates are made to wait for hours before the interview commences in an effort to determine their ability to persevere. In one interview conducted by a telecommunications firm, several candidates were invited for an interview in the morning and were made to wait for about nine hours, by which time just one candidate was still waiting. He got the job!

## The Presentation Interview

The Presentation Interview is usually an integral part of the other types of interviews, especially the Panel Interview or the Group Interview, and is usually done for managerial and senior positions. The purpose is to determine your confidence level, ability to engage an audience, communication skills, and maturity.

In making a good presentation, have a single theme in your message and don't try to sell too many ideas in your presentation or speech. Your audience can't remember too many things, so sum up your speech in a theme that you can repeat in the course of your presentation. Don't be like a catalog, selling many things, unless that is the specific requirement of your presentation.

Engage your audience in your presentation, get some perspectives from them and show empathy. Let your presentation be conversational.

*Notes on Presentations*

## Essential Elements of Good Communication

1. The Sender: You!

2. The Receiver: Your audience (prospects, colleagues, boss, family, friends, etc.)

3. The Message: The theme or core of what you want to communicate to the receiver.

4. The Medium: The vehicle through which the message is sent to your audience (word of mouth, mail, telephone, mass media, etc.).

5. Feedback: Communication is two-way traffic; there is no communication until the receiver understands the message from the sender and provides a response.

6. The most important skill for good communication is listening. Paying attention to your audience is key to successful selling and people engagement. Listen more than you talk to show you care and that the other person is important to you.

No matter how accustomed you are to presentations, you will always have a feeling of anxiety because of the flow of adrenaline in your system, which will typically make you speak faster than you usually do. Consequently, when making a presentation, try to speak slowly and deliberately so your audience can assimilate your message.

*Eloquence and Message*
Don't mistake eloquence of presentation or speech for a great presentation. While eloquence is important for good delivery, it is just a small part of what makes a great presentation. Your speech is only great to the extent that your audience understands what you are communicating and that it provokes the action you desire of them. If the receiver does not assimilate the message, then the purpose of the presentation is not met.

*Being True to Yourself*
The other guidelines you need in making a good presentation include being yourself. If you are not comfortable with humor, don't force it. Let your humor come naturally.

Unless the presentation message is part of you, it will never carry the impelling, moving effect of a good presentation, the kind that brings the audience to its feet. Become the message you want to deliver.

Be dynamic, moderate your gestures so that they don't become a distraction, and make use of the space you have. (Taking one or two steps to "own the space" will help your composure.)

Use metaphors or illustrations where necessary in your presentation. A brief story can help, but remember to distill the essence of the story to convey your message.

Summarize at the end of your presentation. A good presentation is one in which you tell your audience at the beginning what you intend to tell them, then go on to tell them what you want to tell them, and wrap up by telling them what you have told them.

# Appendix E

# Dress Code for Job Interviews

**Dressing for a Professional Interview**

To make the best impression here is more on what to wear:

**Business Attire for Interviews**

*Women*

- Solid color, conservative suit (navy, black or dark grey) with coordinated blouse, the suit skirt should be long enough so you can sit down comfortably, moderate shoes, tan or light pantyhose, and limited jewelry (no dangling earrings or arms full of bracelets).
- Neat, professional hairstyle, manicured nails, light make-up, little or no perfume.
- Portfolio, decent folder or briefcase.

*Men*

- Solid color, conservative suit (solid color—navy or dark grey), long sleeve shirt (white, sky blue or coordinated with the suit), conservative tie, dark socks, and professional shoes.

- Neat hairstyle, trimmed nails, little or no cologne or after-shave.
- Portfolio, decent folder or briefcase.

## Business Casual Dressing

This can mean different things to different employers. There is no strict definition of the phrase. In some cases, business casual attire means pressed khakis/chinos and a button-down long-sleeved shirt. To other companies, it might mean dress jeans and a polo shirt. In general, the following is appropriate attire for interviewing and for dressing in business casual.

Here are helpful tips:

*Women*

- Khaki, corduroy, twill or cotton pants or skirts, neatly pressed.
- Sweaters, twinsets, cardigans, polo/knit shirts.
- Solid colors work better than bright patterns.

*Men*

- Khaki, gabardine or cotton pants, neatly pressed.
- Cotton long-sleeved button-down shirts, pressed, polo shirts or knit shirts with a collar.
- Sweaters.
- Leather shoes and belt.
- Tie is optional.

## What Not to Wear

Regardless of gender, when the dress code is business casual it's not appropriate to wear your favorite old t-shirt, ripped jeans and vintage sneakers. Keep in mind the "business" part of business casual.

## Interview Accessories

When wearing accessories to an interview, less is more. It's important not to overdo the accessories and also important to choose accessories that will enhance your interview attire—not overwhelm it.

*Jewelry*

Women should avoid dangling earrings and arms full of bracelets, and men should wear little or no jewelry other than a watch and/or wedding band. No jewelry is better than cheap or loud jewelry. When it comes to piercings and tattoos, depending on where you are being interviewed, you may want to consider covering your tattoos and taking out your rings.

*Hats*

Don't wear a hat to a job interview regardless of the type of job you are applying for. Don't also wear hoodies or any other type of sweatshirt or sweatpants.

*Shoes*

Don't wear flip-flops or sneakers. You won't make a good impression. Also avoid really high heels and platform shoes. Closed toe shoes in a neutral color are best for women. For men, slip-on or lace-up dress shoes are the best bet.

*Belts*

If your pants or slacks have belt loops, wear a belt. It will tie your outfit together. Your belt should match your outfit and/or your shoes and bag.

*Pantyhose*

The question of whether women should wear pantyhose could be controversial in some cultures but on a scale neutral pantyhose works well.

*Hair and Make Up*

Less is more when it comes to hair and make up. Be subtle and don't over do it with make up. Keep your hair style simple. The same holds true for nail polish. Your nails shouldn't be overly long and your nail polish shouldn't be too bright a color. You don't want the interviewer to even notice your nail color; the focus at all times should be on what you are saying rather than what you are wearing.

*Perfume and Cologne*

You should be conservative with your perfume or cologne. Some people are more sensitive to smell than others. Scent being one of the strongest senses may not work in your favour sometimes; your favorite perfume or cologne might be the same the interviewer's quarrelsome neighbor wore! Don't let subliminal negative impact ruin your chances at getting a job. In this case, less, if not none, is better.

*Portfolio/Purse*

A portfolio is a great accessory. You can store extra copies of your resume, your credentials and your list of references. Or, you may want to consider a large purse or a small briefcase that can hold all your belongings, and what you need for the interview. Regardless of which option you select, always stick to neutral colors,

## Now That You Have an Offer Dress Appropriately for Your Workplace

After you have accepted the job offer, you may be working in an environment where business casual or just plain casual is appropriate workplace attire. If you're not sure what you should wear, ask. There is no better way to make a bad impression than to show up for your first day of work standing out like a sore thumb because you're not dressed correctly.

One reason that it's important to ask, is that you could have interviewed on a dress-down work day, so, don't assume that the way you see people dressed is how you should dress on the

## Appendix F

# Important Tips for Writing an Interview Winning Resume

**1. Choose a Simple Font**

When writing a resume it's important to use a basic font that is easy to read, both for hiring managers and for applicant management systems used by some companies.

Since many of the resumes these days are read by the applicant tracking systems, not by people, bear in mind that the systems work best reading text rather than fancy formatting.

It's also important for the hiring manager to be able to easily read your resume. Using between 10 and 12 point font will ensure that your resume is read. Basic fonts like Arial, Times New Roman, Verdana, Courier and Calibri are usually a good choice. Consider making section headers a little larger and/or bold using 16-20 point font.

Don't overuse capitalization, bold, italics, underlines, or other emphasizing features. Again, basic works best. Be consistent in your formatting. For example, if you bold one section heading, bold all section headings. If you bold the company name, be sure the others are all bold, as well.

## 2. Incorporate All Your Contact Information

It's important to include all your contact information on your resume so employers can easily get in touch with you. Include your full name, street address, city, state, and zip (where applicable), home phone number, cell phone number, and email address.

Use a personal email address, not your work email address. If you don't have a personal email account, create one today. Check the email account frequently, so you can respond to employer inquiries in a timely manner.

It's important to have voicemail or an answering machine so hiring managers can leave a message when you're not available. Let your voicemail message sound professional.

## 3. Incorporate Keywords in Job Description

Your resume should include the same keywords that appear in job descriptions because hiring managers in companies that use recruitment management software search for these keywords. That way, you will increase your chances of your resume matching available positions—and of you being selected for an interview. Also include same keywords in your cover letter.

Your resume keywords should include specific job requirements, including your skills, competencies (professional), relevant credentials, and previous employers.

The best way to find keywords to use in your resume is to use a job search engine to search for job listings. Check the results to see if you can find a common theme in the keywords listed in the job postings. Every job position has its keywords generally used in the industry or for that position and it's your responsibility to find and use them appropriately.

## 4. Choose the Right Resume Format

There are several basic types of resumes used to apply for job openings. Depending on the peculiarity of your circumstances, choose a *chronological* (or sequential), a *functional*, a *combination*, or a *targeted* resume and then take the time to customize it.

*Chronological Resume*

A chronological resume starts by listing your work history, with the most recent position listed first.

Your jobs are listed in reverse chronological order with your current, or most recent job, first. Your education, skills, and other information are listed after your experience. Employers typically prefer this type of resume because it's easy to see what jobs you have held with their respective dates.

*Functional Resume*

A functional resume focuses on your skills and experience rather than on your chronological work history. This resume type is used most often by people who are changing careers or have gaps in their employment history.

*Combination Resume*

A combination resume lists your skills and experience first. Your employment history is listed next in chronological order.

When you use a combination resume you can highlight the skills you have that are relevant to the job you are applying for, and also provide the chronological work history that most employers prefer.

*Targeted Resume*

A targeted resume focuses on a specific job opening. The targeted resume is customized so that it specifically highlight the skills and experiences you have that are relevant to the job you are applying for. Targeted resumes should be edited or rewritten for each job you apply for. It definitely takes more time to write a targeted resume, but it's worth the effort, especially when applying for jobs that are a perfect match for your qualifications and experience. It gives about the best result.

To customize your resume, edit your resume so your skills and experience are as close a match as possible to the job description or job ad requirements. Take the keywords used in the job posting and work them into your resume. This way, your resume will have a much better chance getting selected for consideration.

*Custom Resume*

A custom resume is much the same as a targeted resume and specifically highlights the experiences you have that are relevant to the job you are applying for.

*Resume with Profile*

You can have a resume with a profile section where you include a summary of your skills, experiences, and goals as they relate to the job you are applying for. This gives a snapshot of all the good reasons why you should be shortlisted for the interview. This usually precedes all the detailed information contained in the other parts of the resume.

*Time Gaps in Resume*

Make sure if you have time gaps in employment, you address them in your resume. Time gaps are often flagged as a concern by recruiters and technology. Some experts suggest listing only years of employment to cover up employment gaps, such as 2007-2009, but the intelligent recruiting management systems will typically flag this.

You are better off explaining employment gaps: taking on independent consulting or freelancing positions, taking time off to have a child, or taking a pretty long vocation to refresh alongside the relevant dates. If a candidate took classes or went back to school, list the appropriate information in the education section.

## 5. Use A Resume Template

If you need to create or enhance your resume, using a resume template is a good starting point. It's always useful to review resume templates and samples when you are writing your resume, so you can get an idea of what a resume should look like.

Add your information to the resume template, then tweak and edit it to personalize your resume, so it highlights your skills and abilities.

It can be helpful to use a template to get started writing a resume and cover letters. Google Docs or Microsoft Word have a variety of free resume and cover letter templates job seekers can use as a starting point to create resumes and letters.

## 6. Prioritize Your Resume Content

It's important to prioritize the content of your resume so that your most important and relevant experience is listed first, with key accomplishments listed against each position.

You should prioritize your accomplishments (as you compile your resume) by importance and relevance to the job you're applying for.

*Decide What's Relevant*

To decide what's relevant, put yourself in the position of a potential employer and ask if the information on your resume can convince the employer that you are a worthwhile candidate to interview for the position they are trying to fill.

*Prioritize the Details*

Next, prioritize the information you provide in each description. Present what you think is of greatest interest to your prospective employer first. For instance, consider a candidate seeking a job in a retail store. The resume might reflect an experience in which 30% of the candidate's time was spent on the sales floor in a current or previous employment, and 70% was spent in inventory management in the store. Priority, determined by relevance to the employer, dictates that sales floor experience should be listed before the store inventory management.

In addition, quantify as much information as you can—numbers, currency signs, percentages attract attention and can position you to be selected for the interview.

As you compile statements for your resume, prioritize them by importance, noteworthiness and relevance to the job.

Include a concise mission statement about yourself and the type of position you seek near the top of your resume that is matched to your targeted position and goes beyond generic phrases such as, "Seeking challenging job in a fun yet hard-working environment," or "Seeking a job in a dynamic environment where I can add value and make a difference." You must go beyond these clichés if you want your resume to rise above the pack.

7. **Tailor Your Resume Objective**

If you include an objective on your resume, it's important to tailor your resume objective to match the job you are applying for. The more specific you are, the better chance you have of being considered for the job you are interested in. Many don't review the objective on their resume and some may even forget what it says though its very conspicuous on the first page of their resume; resist the temptation of using same objective for all jobs you apply for, exercise the discipline to tailor this objective to the job.

Some job seekers choose to include an objective on their resume, rather than including it in the body of their cover letter. Where you include the objective is optional, but including a resume objective can convince employers that you know what you want and are familiar with the job, the industry, and the company.

For details of resume objectives please visit www.harrynnoli.com.

## 8. Leverage Technology

The job market is highly competitive, therefore you need to make sure that your resume rises above the pack, in a professional way that shows you have taken the time and interest to pursue a specific job opening. Most recruitment management software in use search for keywords as earlier discussed and to ensure you optimize your resume insert these professional keywords of the job description

Write your resume concisely, proofreading to avoid typos and errors, using active verbs to hype your skills and accomplishments

*Use Social Media*

Employers are increasingly looking in many different online places for talent, including Facebook, Yookos, MySpace, LinkedIn, and other social networking sites. Make sure when you are in the market for a new job you use all of your online profiles to help position yourself as an ideal job candidate.

Networking can be surprisingly fruitful on these types of sites, so whenever appropriate, make reference to previous employers, job titles, dates of employment and responsibilities. Let your connections know you are looking for a new job so you can get contacted on new opportunities. And always make sure there is nothing on your public profiles that you wouldn't want a prospective employer to see.

## Important Tips Before Sending Your Email Resume

If the job posting asks you to send an attachment, send your resume as a PDF or a Word document. If you have word processing software other than Microsoft Word save your resume as a Word (.doc) document. File, Save As, should be an option in your program.

To save your document as a PDF, depending on your word processing software you may be able to File, Print to Adobe PDF. If not, there are programs you can use to convert a file to a PDF, any good search engine can help you with this.

Some employers do not accept attachments. In these cases, paste your resume into your email message as plain text. Use a simple font and remove the fancy formatting. Don't use HTML. You don't know what email client the employer is using, so, simple is best because the employer may not see a formatted message the same way you do.

*The Subject Line of Your Email Message*

Make sure you list the position you are applying for in the Subject line of your email address, so the employer is clear as to what job you are applying for.

*Include Your Signature*

Include a signature with your contact information, so it's easy for the hiring manager to get in touch with you.

*Double Check Your Email Message*

Make sure you spell check and check your grammar and capitalization. They are just as important in email messages as in paper correspondence.

*Send a Test Email Message*

Attach your resume, and then send the message to yourself first to test that the formatting works. Open the attachment so you are sure you attached the right file in the right format and it opens correctly. If everything looks good, send to the employer.

## Appendix G

# Benefits of SWOT Analysis

When using SWOT analysis it helps you identify the issues or problems you intend to change, set goals and create an action plan.

SWOT is a simple yet comprehensive way of assessing the positive and negative forces within and without an organization. The more information you have at your disposal and the more knowledgeable people you involve in preparing the SWOT, the more valuable your analysis will be.

It helps you see how to build on your strengths, minimize your weaknesses, seize opportunities and counteract threats. It will reveal the gaps you can close and areas for action.

For individuals attending an interview, it helps you clearly see and define what you can help the prospective employer achieve based on the strengths that you possess and the opportunities they have in the marketplace.

The table below succinctly illustrates SWOT analysis:

|  |  | **Positive** | **Negative** |
|---|---|---|---|
|  |  | Helpful to achieving objectives | Harmful to achieving objectives |
| **Internal** | (Attributes of the organization) | **S**trengths | **W**eaknesses |
| **External** | (Attributes of the environment) | **O**pportunities | **T**hreats |

Appendix **H**

# A Simple Breathing Exercise to Relieve Tension

Do this a minute or two before a performance or before facing an interview panel:

1. Take a deep breath and hold for five seconds or the count of five. Feel the pressure in your lungs.

2. Slowly, and gently, and deliberately breathe out over a count of seven to ten seconds.

3. Repeat steps 1 and 2 three times.

This exercise will have a calming effect on you. Use it any time you are nervous before a performance. It has always worked for me.

You could also attempt to do anything that distracts you or takes your attention away from the immediate task of a presentation/speech. For example, dropping your pen and picking it up or sharing a joke with a friend moments before a speech could help minimize your anxiety.

# Bibliography

1. Beshara, Tony. 2008. "Acing the Interview: How to Ask and Answer the Questions that Will Get You the Job." AMACOM, Division of American Management Association

2. Brian Platz. "Resume Writing Tips for a Technology-Savvy World." http://www.about.com

3. Byrne, Rhonda. 2006. The Secret: Atria Books.

4. Covey, Stephen. 2004. The $8^{th}$ Habit: From Effectiveness to Greatness. New York: Free Press.

5. Doyle, Allison. "Interview Questions and Answers." http://www.about.com/od/interviewquestionsanswers.

6. Frankel, Barbara. "Interview Best Practices." Career Counselors Consortium. http://www.careercc.org.

7. Greene, Kera. "Interview Best Practices." Career Counselors Consortium. www.careercc.org.

8. Hill, Napoleon; Cornwell, Ross. 2004. Think and Grow Rich, The Original Version, Restored and Revised. San Diego, CA: Aventine Press.

9. Tracy, Brian. 2004. The Psychology of Selling. Nashville, Tennessee: Thomas Nelson Inc.

10. Welch, Jack, and Suzy Welch. 2005. Winning. New York: Harper Collins.

## About the Author

Harry Ike Nnoli is a management consultant, business philosopher, and motivational speaker. He has more than twenty years of experience in marketing, sales, and business management. He has worked in roles up to the chief executive management level in multinational corporations across diverse industries. He is the founder of Smiles Training & Consulting and host of the motivational program, *Positive Difference*, which appears on radio and other platforms and inspires listeners to become their best, irrespective of circumstances. He brings a balanced perspective to personal and professional development.

## About the Book

*You're Hired* guides young professionals toward making the best of job interviews. It recognizes that a candidate's qualifications can get him or her through the interviewer's door, but securing the dream job requires much more.

This book provides the three key strategies for getting hired. It shows how to identify the strongest qualities a candidate has for any job interview and additionally, provides the most appropriate responses to typical job interview questions. This material comes with practice worksheets to help the candidate apply the key learning of the book and position him or her perfectly for the next dream job.

# Audio Materials for Personal Development

**Positive Difference Classics**

The ***Classics***, is a collection of some of the best of the radio motivational and personal development programme, *Positive Difference*. This ten-track CD comprises of titles like *the Secret of Top Achievers, Never Give Up, Be Known for something, and Avoiding Failure*.

**Enter The Future of Your Dreams**

This nine–track CD is a collection of thoughts on the all-important subject of Purpose and Vision with titles like *Beauty of Purpose, Destiny Beckons, and Writing Your Personal Vision Plan among others*. This material helps you navigate through the clutter of everyday activities to focus on the important tasks that are connected to your vision.

**Discover Your Strength—Talent Not Enough**

This eleven-track CD demystifies the subject of talent and gift and shows you how to discover, refine and serve them to the world. It has titles like *Be an Original, Steps to Discover your Strength and Talents, Develop Your Talent* and *Find Your Passion*.

**You Are Hired**

This CD provides a summary of the book, *You're Hired*. It provides the three key strategies for getting hired and shows how to identify your strongest qualities for any job interview. Additionally, it provides you with the most appropriate responses to typical job interview questions and offers perspectives on career and job choices.

# Coming Soon!

## Grow Rich! The Secrets of the Rich

Find out the timeless formula for success and accumulating riches based on over 20 years of study of the ancient and contemporary wealthy individuals. If you desire to accumulate wealth and leave your mark on the sands of time then this book is for you.

For more, visit www.harrynnoli.com